GIFTS
OF THE
EUCHARIST

Stories to Transform
and Inspire

NANCY C. REEVES
BERNADETTE GASSLEIN

ave maria press **AmP** notre dame, indiana

© 2009 by Nancy C. Reeves and Bernadette Gasslein

Founded in 1865, Ave Maria Press is a ministry of the Indiana Province of Holy Cross.

www.avemariapress.com

ISBN-10 1-59471-203-4   ISBN-13 978-1-59471-203-6

Cover and text design by John R. Carson.

Cover photo © Ian Shaw / Alamy.

Printed and bound in the United States of America.

Library of Congress Cataloging-in-Publication Data
    Reeves, Nancy Christine, 1952
    Gifts of the Eucharist : stories to transform and inspire / Nancy C. Reeves, Bernadette Gasslein.
        p. cm.
    ISBN-13: 978-1-59471-203-6
    ISBN-10: 1-59471-203-4
    1. Lord's Supper--Catholic Church. 2. Spiritual life--Catholic Church. I. Gasslein, Bernadette. II. Title.
    BX2215.3.R44 2009
    234'.163--dc22
                                                2008047919

CONTENTS

DEDICATION

To the members of the Archdiocese of Regina Eucharistic Congress Committee, who asked for seven lenten missions on the eucharist, and suggested that a booklet be written to go with the presentations. This book grew out of that vision.

To everyone who told us their stories about the power of the eucharist.

To all who have shared at the table with us, in joy and in pain: Thank you.

PREFACE

Jesus established the celebration we now call the eucharist when—in the course of a Passover celebration—he blessed the bread and the cup, gave them to his followers and said, "Do this in remembrance of me." Over two thousand years later, we are still doing eucharist in remembrance of Jesus. But describing the eucharistic celebration in this way runs the risk of limiting our understanding of its power. Saying we attend Mass to remember what Jesus did can leave us with the impression that we are the key participants, offering Christ our love, thanksgiving, and praise. Of course we do this, yet the eucharist is a ritual celebration in which we also receive abundant gifts from our three-personed God.

We are both passionate about the eucharist and what it means for our lives as individuals and for the countless people who have shared their faith stories with us. I, Nancy, am a clinical psychologist and spiritual director, and Bernadette is a catechist, workshop facilitator, and editor. We are both published authors. Over the years we have heard many inspiring stories from the recipients of many spiritual gifts that God has graciously given during worship. This book explores ten of these gifts: transformation, remembrance, thanksgiving, reconciliation, healing, nourishment, guidance, embrace, community, and celebration. Drawing on our personal and professional experiences, we utilize the following tools for growth in this book as we explore each of these gifts.

- Stories and quotes from adults and youth who, while attending Mass, received direction, comfort, love, courage, forgiveness, or whatever gift they needed for their life journey
- Spiritual information and psychological principles about how to become more receptive to the gifts of the eucharist
- Questions and exercises to explore individually or in groups, aimed at helping you, the reader, enter more fully into the eucharist and live more deeply.

Our hope is that the stories and information we share here will remind you of the gifts God has given you through the eucharist, and that you will become even more receptive to the present and future gifts that you are being offered.

Abundant blessings,
Nancy and Bernadette

* * *

Singer/songwriter Linnea Good frequently presents with Dr. Nancy Reeves. She has composed a short chant for each "gift." Words and music can be found on her website: www.linneagood.com.

ONE

TRANSFORMATION

The purpose of celebrating the liturgy is not to give lip service to God, but to glorify him as Jesus glorified him. We do this by transforming our lives under the influence of the Spirit of Jesus so that we become increasingly Christ-like in our total devotion to God and to the welfare of others.

—Mark Searle
Liturgy Made Simple, p. 64

In their consideration of the actuosa participatio *[active participation] of the faithful in the liturgy, the synod fathers also discussed the personal conditions required for fruitful participation on the part of individuals. One of these is certainly the spirit of constant conversion, which must mark the lives of all the faithful. Active participation in the eucharistic liturgy can hardly be expected if one approaches it superficially, without an examination of his or her own life.*

—Pope Benedict XVI, *Sacramentum Caritatis,* 55

1

Spiritual Transformation

So much of the spiritual life is about transformation. Transformation is not just change: It is radical change. As we age, we develop attitudes and patterns that move us toward God and others that move us in the opposite direction. Maturing in our faith means being open to the refining power of the Holy Spirit in our lives. It means surrendering to the action of Christ, who draws us more deeply into the life of the Trinity in which he participates intimately. This surrender means letting go of those things that disfigure the image of God within us.

It means becoming more Christ-like, which paradoxically means becoming more ourselves—our deep, inner selves. Becoming fully human is a challenge that is lived out between two poles. We must not be afraid to be fully who we are, and we must not overstep our graced, creaturely existence and succumb to the ancient temptation of putting ourselves in the place of God. Drawn into the life of God in the eucharist, we see clearly who we are; at the same time the eucharist illuminates any sinfulness in our lives, calling us to put it aside so that we might live the fullness of God's life. "To err is human" is not an adequate definition of humanity. We too often fail to recognize that sin reduces our humanity. Being drawn into the life of grace leads us to full, vibrant humanity—in the image of Jesus, who was fully human and fully divine.

Every eucharistic celebration speaks overtly about our need for transformation and God's longing for us to accept the help offered. Transformation can be difficult, painful, and embarrassing, and yet sometimes it gives us a feeling of freedom even while it is occurring. When God invites us into a process of transformation, it goes more smoothly if we have already given God *carte blanche* to refine us. Linda Leone has done so and wrote these thoughts about the experience:

> I have found inspiration in many of the homilies of Father John Joliffe when he was at St. Joseph's Parish. One in particular stood out for me. The homily was regarding Mark 12:17. Jesus tells the Pharisees, "Give unto Caesar what is Caesar's and give unto God what is God's." Father John updated this by saying that we, too, must decide what we are giving to God in terms of time, presence, and prayer. "Caesar" in Father John's homily was all the time we give to work or things that distract us from having a relationship with God.
>
> This spoke to me at the time. I had been struggling with how much time I spent at work. My prayer time was nonexistent. As I prayed after the eucharist, I realized that my work could also be part of my ministry to God—how I did my work, how I brought prayer and gratitude to my workplace would give unto God what was God's. This homily was transformative! Because of it, I changed how I was living my daily life.
>
> When I feel like I am getting too distracted with work or responsibilities, I still remind myself to give to Caesar what is Caesar's, and to give to God what is God's. This puts my focus back on God. I slow down, pray a bit, and continue. I work in a public institution; often my prayers are

private, or I find ways to say the prayer in a meeting. For example, I might say in a humorous tone
when we are problem-solving something, "Oh,
bless us with wisdom!" No one seems to mind my
spontaneous mini-prayers.

We have heard many folks say, "I can't believe that
homily this morning! I'm sure it was created just for
me!" And we have talked with a number of priests
who say much the same thing. As they pray about the
upcoming scripture readings, they may experience a
divine nudge that directs them to a particular piece
of information, or they see a particular parishioner
or issue in the community linked with the readings.
Some have even thrown out their prepared homily
when the Spirit gives them a particular nudge as they
are getting ready to speak! Our God is always aware
of our immediate concerns. It is no surprise, then,
when members of the congregation express gratitude
for the personal guidance and support they received.

Of course, our God is the only true multi-tasker,
and can speak to each heart just what it needs to
hear. During Mass, a scripture passage, prayer, or
homily may have 230 different meanings to match
the spiritual needs of each of the 230 members of the
congregation. In this story, however, God gave the
same meaning to all, which provided a wake-up call
to a church family who had previously been rather
disconnected from the eucharist. The following story
is from Fr. Kevin Lynch, O.F.M.

It was when the Moose Jaw, Saskatchewan, mili-
tary base was to lose its defense budget and there
was a concern about jobs. As it turned out the

NATO forces contracted the base to train pilots with a budget that covered all the previous jobs (it was in the billion-dollar range). So there was great rejoicing in the local community.

The Sunday after this breakthrough was announced, I had occasion to preach in a parish that never took much part in the liturgy. Trying to be faithful to the Gospel that brings peace, I proclaimed that the billions of dollars could have been used for hockey arenas, curling rinks, libraries, theatres, opera houses, etc. in the local community, and it would also have created jobs. The whole congregation participated very enthusiastically from then on. There is a real presence in the Word of the Lord. As the presider, I knew that I had connected with all the people of God who had gathered to hear the Word.

This congregation was thrown off balance by Fr. Kevin's homily. And they accepted the Word they heard, which changed their subsequent experience of eucharist. We have heard of many incidences when people have felt disoriented or thrown off balance by a divine invitation. St. Paul even fell off his horse! God provides the impetus, yet we always have the choice to fall into God or to fall more deeply into ourselves.

Transformation is a life-long process. Many people are disappointed when they experience a major breakthrough in attitudes or behaviors, only to revert to old patterns a short time later. Yet this is the usual way of it. We humans often need repetition to let a new way of being take hold. For example, trust may be one of your issues. It may be difficult to trust God, other people, or yourself. You might have felt betrayed by someone in your past. God will be patient with you and will keep bringing this issue to your attention as you slowly learn to trust in a healthy way. Meeting God through the eucharist, on a regular basis, is one way we say "yes" to ongoing refinement.

My name is Ron Turner, and for many years I was a somewhat lost soul looking for some direction and light. I was raised in an anti-Catholic home and was quite prejudiced without realizing it. Although I did not realize it at the time, the Lord had his hand on me ever since I was ten years old, and I invited him into my life by saying the sinner's prayer along with a radio evangelist one night. I was on cloud nine for two or three days but had no one I could trust to tell of the new love for the Lord I was bursting with.

There was a forty-year dry spell between that very significant event and the next very significant event when the Lord reached down and rescued me from the toxic spiritual path I had taken. I experienced a vision where I was surrounded by crosses like a picket fence! I was so damaged by all the negative beliefs I had that it took many months of listening to Christian radio before I could even bring myself to pray, and six years before I could drag myself through the doors of a church. Jesus was my lifeline during that time.

In the Church, I discovered Jesus in the eucharist. Since I became a Catholic, I have received much healing and guidance during the Mass. I remember the second time I went to Mass, I was still pretty nervous. During the reading of the Gospel, the crucifer, torch bearers, and priest looked like they were under a spotlight, but there were no lights to be seen and it was a dull day. It was a beautiful reassurance for me of the Lord's presence. It calmed me down.

My major conversion experience happened after a homily in which the priest talked of the spiritual benefits of spending an hour on your knees in front of the tabernacle. I did as he suggested, and it was like someone opened a furnace door. Major heat! And I was there for an hour. It was so healing. Since then I have always felt his glorious presence in the tabernacle and on the altar. Praise God! Joining the Church started out as a really rough ride, but it is beautiful now. Thank you, Jesus.

FEAR OF THE LORD

In the story you just read, Ron was frightened of God for a long time. Jesus needed to woo him slowly for years before he could set foot in a church. One impediment to our transformation is the belief that God wants to be feared. You have probably heard the following scriptures many times during Mass.

> Who are they that fear the Lord?
> He will teach them the way
> that they should choose.
> They will abide in prosperity,
> and their children shall possess the land.
> The friendship of the Lord is
> for those who fear him,
> and he makes his covenant known
> to them. (Ps 25:12–14)

O taste and see that the Lord is good;
happy are those who take refuge in him.
O fear the Lord, you his holy ones;
for those who fear him have no want. (Ps 34:8–9)

The fear of the Lord is the beginning of wisdom;
all those who practice it have
a good understanding
His praise endures forever. (Ps 111:10)

Praise the Lord!
Happy are those who fear the Lord,
who greatly delight in his commandment.
Their descendants will be mighty in the land;
the generation of the upright will
be blessed. (Ps 112:1–2)

We don't usually associate fear with the benefits mentioned in these psalms—love, happiness, healing, security, and abundance. Fear in a human partner usually results in restriction, pain, and dissatisfaction with the relationship. So, how could fearing God be positive for us—or for God? Would you want your loved ones to fear you? Of course not. Then why would God repeatedly ask for our fear through the mouth of prophet after prophet?

On the other hand, we read that when the angel Gabriel appeared to Mary, her response was to be "much perplexed." Seeing this, the angel said to her, "Do not be afraid, Mary, for you have found favor with God" (Lk 1:30). And, when the priest Zechariah was "filled with the Holy Spirit" and prophesied about his baby son, who was to be called John the Baptist, he spoke of the divine-human covenant:

Thus he has shown the mercy
promised to our ancestors,
and has remembered his holy covenant,
the oath that he swore to our ancestor Abraham,
to grant us that we, being rescued
from the hands of our enemies,
might serve him without fear, in
holiness and righteousness
before him all our days. (Lk 1:72–75)

And one night, shepherds were watching their flocks in the hills above Bethlehem. Then an angel of the Lord stood before them, and the glory of the Lord shone around them, and they were terrified. But the angel said to them, "Do not be afraid; for see—I am bringing you good news of great joy for all the people." (Lk 2:9–10)

To explore this concept of fear of the Lord, let us consider the meaning of the word "fear." The *Oxford American Dictionary* defines fear as "an unpleasant emotion caused by the belief that someone or something is dangerous, likely to cause pain, or a threat." We experience danger when our body, mind, emotions, or spirit are put at risk. The fear of the Lord, however, has different meanings. *Vine's Complete Expository Dictionary of Old and New Testament Words* speaks of fear of the Lord as a "wholesome dread" of displeasing God, rather than a fear of divine "power and righteous retribution." The *HarperCollins Bible Dictionary* describes fear of the Lord as "the awe that a person ought to have before God," while the *Collegeville Pastoral Dictionary of Biblical Theology* reports a number of different meanings for or associations with the expression: being fearful; reverential fear; retreat from God; a response to the power of a theophany (such as the burning bush in the Old Testament, or the story of the transfiguration in the Gospels of Mark and Matthew); fear of death from being in the presence of God; obedience to God's commands; loving and serving the Lord; an impetus to praise the Lord; a partner with holiness and a reminder of our dependence on God.

Can we feel love and fear at the same time? Most of us, no doubt, know from experience that we can. I remember holding my newborn daughter and feeling my heart melt with love. Then I had a stab of fear with the thought, "She is so precious. How could I ever give her all she deserves?" Similarly, Allan told me that he experienced such intense love for God one day after receiving communion that he thought he would physically die. He said, "Part of me was terrified by this thought, yet part of me longed to lose myself totally in the love, even if death were the end result."

Although this feeling of fear may arise at times in our relationships with others and our relationship with God, it usually doesn't last long. Generally such a feeling is part of the experience of awe, which is a feeling of reverential respect mixed with fear or wonder (*Oxford American Dictionary*). An experience moves out of the ordinary and elicits feelings of awe when we give our full attention to it. Have you ever idly watched a butterfly and then suddenly become aware of a child's rapt attention to the fluttering insect? The child's connection to the butterfly is so full that the result is awe, while you only experience a mild enjoyment. The more of ourselves we give to an experience, the more we are likely to receive. Jesus told his followers, "Pay attention to what you hear; the measure you give will be the measure you get, and still more will be given you" (Mk 4:24).

When we live the first commandment, loving God with our body, mind, heart, and spirit, we encourage awe, with its mixture of fear and wonder. At times we will experience wonder and at other times, fear. The fear, though, is not of God's actions. The fear arises when we perceive a threat to our "status quo," our existing state. Change comes with the experience of awe, and part of us does not want to change. Another part of us, though, realizes that the divine invitation is for us to become new creations, refined and transformed by love. Every time we take the bread of life and every time we drink the cup of salvation, God invites us to die and rise again with Jesus.

The flash of fear that comes with awe can help us realize how precious God is to us, and it reminds us that God has relinquished power over us by giving us free will. We are loved so much that we have the freedom to accept or reject God's invitation to refinement and transformation.

The fear becomes unhealthy, though, if we don't allow it to transform into wonder. Living in fear binds us, keeping our focus on how sinful we are. When we hold onto fear, we wait for God to act in threatening or punishing ways toward us, and we attend Mass not as beloved children giving thanks for the sacrifice of Jesus, but as sinful creatures who will be judged harshly by the Judge. This view, as well as harming our self-esteem, distorts the reality of God.

The First Letter of John speaks to this issue: "God is love, and those who abide in love abide in God, and

God abides in them. Love has been perfected among us in this; that we may have boldness on the day of judgment, because as he is, so are we in this world. There is no fear in love, but perfect love casts out fear; for fear has to do with punishment, and whoever fears has not reached perfection in love" (4:16b–18). The Holy Spirit transforms our fear into wonder and love, helping us move from bondage to freedom.

God is exquisitely sensitive to our feelings and concerns and encourages us to move quickly past the fear component of awe. Repeatedly, the Lord invites us to psychological health—to giving and receiving love in the absence of anything that will restrict or diminish either partner. God does this by self-revelation. And the eucharist is all about self-revelation. Through scripture, through taking the body and blood of Christ, through the homily, and through the action of the Holy Spirit working in us through the Mass, we are invited to grow closer to God. As we experience God's reality through the eucharist, the distorted, hurtful images and beliefs about our Creator can be transformed. Then, as we experience the fear of the Lord, it is an awe-filled wonder that benefits us rather than a dysfunctional fear that restricts us. We are then better able to cherish the reality of our God.

The Ultimate Question

Sometimes allowing transformation is a choice between living in a more or less restricted manner. Sometimes it means choosing to live or die. Tracy Tomiak has been called to tell the world about her transformative experiences. She is the author of *Thriving Not Just Surviving: Living Abundantly with Pain* (www.painandliving.com) and the founder of www.livingmyfaith.com. She took time out of her busy schedule to write a story for this book.

"Power is made perfect in weakness" (2 Cor 12:9). These are gentle, loving words for a world filled with struggles, pain, and everyday failures. These were Christ's words to me at a time when life seemed hardest. Living with severe chronic pain from a car accident, I could not understand why God would take someone so willing to work for him and make her incapable of performing even the simplest duties of the day. I had used all of my mental, physical, and emotional resources to recover. When all of these were depleted, and I could no longer do it on my own, I leaned on Christ in a way that I had never had to or chosen to before. He showed me his power made perfect in my weakness.

At one of the darkest times of my life, when the pain was overtaking my life and destroying who I was, I drove out of my driveway unsure if I would return. I felt incapable of caring for the needs of my family and thought I was doing more damage than good. This couldn't possibly be God's plan for my life. I drove aimlessly around the city, wondering where to go, and ended up at the only safe place where I knew I could think— our city's perpetual adoration chapel.

As I sat before Christ, he spoke to my heart so deeply, and a peace washed over my entire body. He asked me to rest in him and trust in him alone. He had a plan, and I could trust in that plan or be discouraged about how much my life had changed. He assured me that my family needed me just to be with them and that my value was tied to how much I loved, not how much I could accomplish. My darkness was lifted, and I felt a sense of refreshment and assurance that in Christ I could do all things. For me that meant going forward to live a life of abundance regardless of pain or circumstance.

Being present at Mass and receiving Christ in the eucharist has taught me that my pain is a holy journey filled with purpose and meaning. Christ outlines a path of joy and acceptance that challenges us to embrace life, even under difficult circumstances. Christ continually changes my heart and shows me how great life can be when he is the leader and I am following *his* path for me—not my own. Most importantly, over the years he has taught me to find worthiness in him and not things of the world. Jobs, accolades, promotions, success, and friendships can all crumble, but Christ is the solid ground that is immovable, the solid ground upon which our lives are intended to be built. In each of us lies an empty space that can be filled only with Christ's love. We all desire peace, serenity, and a place of refuge. In wisdom, the Catholic Church has given us this gift. It is found in the beauty and strength of the eucharist—the source and summit of life.

Ongoing Transformation

Transformation is a life-long process. Sometimes we are not aware of how God is working deep within us. Sometimes we are only too aware of an invitation to change a belief, attitude, or behavior that restricts us, yet we cling to it because of its familiarity. A specific transformation may take years or occur much more quickly. We end this chapter with an example of an instantaneous transformation after everyone had given up hope that change could occur.

> I'm Vivian Bosch. As Pastoral Assistant of our parish, I was blessed to assist twenty-six children with their first holy communion. The teachers in our separate school, parents, and parish staff worked together to prepare them. The group included Emma, a child with special needs. The teachers adapted activities especially for her that taught about Jesus in a way that she could understand. As the days drew closer to the celebration, it became evident, however, that this child might not be ready to receive communion because she was finding it difficult to swallow the host.
>
> All the adults involved brainstormed different options, including waiting a year. Over the next few days, as her parents practiced with Emma, we all realized that she just couldn't do it. So, the other adults resigned themselves to trying again next year. As I prayed about it, however, the

passage where Jesus said, "Let the little children come to me" kept repeating itself in my heart. Surely Jesus does mean all twenty-six children! So I told the others that it was right to allow her to try.

On Sunday morning Emma arrived with her family. She wore a beautiful dress, and judging by the look on her face, she understood that this was a very special day for her and her friends. Her smile could not be erased, her blue eyes twinkled, and her rosy, red cheeks expressed much joy. The time came for all the children to receive their first holy communion. Emma and her parents joined in the line to come and receive. When it came her turn, our pastor offered the host to her, saying, "Take it and eat it." Without any hesitation, Emma took and ate!

Her father turned around, looked at me with a big smile on his face that said, "Yes!" What a blessed moment at this eucharistic celebration for all families involved. All twenty-six children who had been preparing to receive Jesus in the eucharist for the first time made their first holy communion. Jesus did for her what we couldn't do. The full meaning of the eucharist, for me, rests on this miraculous abundance that God continues to provide through Jesus.

Closing Prayer

From Psalm 139, with responses by Nancy Reeves

O Lord, you have searched me and known me!
You know when I sit down and when I rise up,
you discern my thoughts from afar (vv. 1–2).

My God, you know me so much better
than I know myself.
You know my strengths and my weaknesses,
and you accept and love all parts of me.

For you formed my inward parts;
you knitted me together in my mother's womb.
I praise you, for I am fearfully and wonderfully
made (vv. 13–14).

Guide me in self-awareness, My God;
so I can truly respect myself
as an awesome work of your hands.

Search me, O God, and know my heart;
test me and know my thoughts.
See if there is any wicked way in me,
and lead me in the way everlasting (vv. 23–24).

You know my weakness so much better than I.
Give me the wisdom and courage to change
what may be changed while I live,
and to accept that some restrictions will not
be lifted until I come home to you.
Amen.

Questions to Journal or Discuss

1. Which story of transformation in this chapter touched you most deeply? Do you know why?
2. Describe a time when you experienced transformation during the eucharist. Was God responding to your request for change? Or, did God's invitation awaken you to a need for transformation?

Spiritual Activity

Choose a personal issue, such as lack of trust or compassion, that needs transformation. Think or write about how it has restricted you over the years. Then, move into prayer and hold it and yourself in God's presence, asking for refinement. Stay in prayer as long as it seems right to you.

After your prayer time, recall incidents when God has already worked on this issue with you. Even if it has only now come to your attention as something in need of transformation, God has been at work on it—sometimes visibly and sometimes invisibly—for years. Get a sense of the flow of the transformative process up to the present. You may find it helpful to write about this process as a list or a flow chart.

Give thanks to God for the refinement that has already occurred, and be grateful for your willingness to be transformed.

* * *

From Linnea Good: "Psalm 118: And On This Path."
Words and music at www.linneagood.com.

two

REMEMBRANCE

When contemporary Catholics celebrate the eucharist, they remember. They experience the eucharist and its call to action in the immediate present. By their remembering, however, they are drawn into communion with all who have celebrated Jesus' victory for the last 2,000 years. Their contemporary experience of the eucharist can be deepened if they understand how the tradition of the past is continually re-appropriated by the present.
—Mary Durkin
The Eucharist, p. 9

The remembrance of [Christ's] perfect gift consists not in the mere repetition of the Last Supper, but in the eucharist itself, that is, in the radical newness of Christian worship.
—Pope Benedict XVI, *Sacramentum Caritatis*, 11

THE ACT OF REMEMBERING

Remembering is a theme that runs through the Bible. For the people of the Hebrew scriptures, remembering is first of all a characteristic of God. The great events of the Exodus that the celebration of Passover commemorates—the defeat of the Egyptians and the liberation of the Hebrew slaves—are kept alive, not just by the remembering of the people, but also by God's remembering. Because God remembers these events—the very foundation of the covenant between God and the Chosen People—these events continue to be alive and effective in the lives of the believers who are likewise caught up in the act of remembering.

"Remember what the Lord has done for you" is a refrain that runs through these scriptures. It is both a stimulus to right action (remember what the Lord has done for you and do likewise) and the very foundation of worship. Worship places before us what God has done for us and prompts us to give thanks. This is true of God's deeds both in the past and in the present. As she prepared to sing a psalm at the Easter Vigil, a cantor who had survived a bout with breast cancer commented, "I can sing this—because it's true." Her Psalm refrain? "I will praise you, Lord, for you have rescued me."

When we pray the eucharist, we are drawn into the process of remembering. From the opening words and gesture of marking our bodies with the cross and calling to mind the Trinity to the end, when we are blessed in the name of that same Trinity, all our words and gestures bring this process of remembering to life in our midst. Hearing the scriptures helps us remember God's activity in the past; the homily invites us to remember how, in our own particular circumstances, God has acted similarly on our behalf. In the creed, we remember and bring to life our baptismal profession of faith. Remembering God's word and action, we intercede for the world in the Prayer of the Faithful.

The Eucharistic Prayer is also full of remembering. We tell the story of Jesus' self-giving on the night before he died. Remembering his death, resurrection, and ascension, we know that we can pray in confidence for the Church and for all who are living and dead. By praying our Great Amen at the end of the Eucharistic Prayer, we remember and affirm our solidarity with Christ's worship. The Lord's Prayer remembers God's bounty and solicitude. And in the greatest act of remembrance, we are drawn into Christ's dying and rising when we share in holy communion. With him, we hand ourselves over to God, joined to his perfect act of surrender. We remember all this during the week as we, who have been sent forth in peace, bring Christ's presence to all we meet.

In worship, we are drawn into the relationship of love between Father (Abba), Son, and Spirit. All of Jesus' teaching shows us the reality of God as Abba, whose desire is for us to say yes to an intentional, intimate, divine-human relationship, and to become partners in bringing about the fullness of the Kingdom. In the eucharist, he moves from teaching to embodiment as his own self-surrender embodies the relationship between Abba, Son, and Spirit. He essentially says, "Look at me, see what I'm doing and you will see who

God is." His self-giving shows us what love looks like in the heart of the Trinity.

For the followers of Jesus, this was a new pattern and a new teaching. When his disciples expressed concern that Jesus would no longer be with them, he said, "I will not leave you orphaned; I am coming to you. In a little while the world will no longer see me, but you will see me; because I live, you also will live. On that day you will know that I am in my Father, and you in me, and I in you" (Jn 14:18–20). Now we experience the presence of his Spirit.

> And I will ask the Father, and he will give you another Advocate, to be with you forever. This is the Spirit of truth, whom the world cannot receive, because it neither sees him nor knows him. You know him, because he abides with you, and he will be in you. (Jn 14:16–17)

This we need to remember: that Christ is not just a prophet, or a wonderful healer, or an inspiring teacher. He is God. Raymond J. Lahey, Bishop of Antigonish, Nova Scotia, spoke poetically about Christ in the Eucharist: "God wanted us to know that in Jesus Christ, truly present among us, heaven is lovingly married to earth, and earth to heaven."

In the eucharist, we meet God as One and as Three. We meet God as Jesus in the bread and wine. We meet Abba God through scripture; we meet the Holy Spirit who transforms our gifts and who transforms us more deeply into the body of Christ as we share in the Lord's body and blood.

When we pray the eucharist in remembrance of Jesus, we remember who God truly is—Father, Son, and Holy Spirit—and that we are in relationship with these three persons of the Holy Trinity. We come face to face with the reality of our unconditionally loving God and know ourselves beloved. So, as Mary Durkin writes in the quote that opens this chapter, "remembering" Jesus is not some sentimental nostalgia for the "good old days" when the incarnate Jesus walked the earth. No, remembering Jesus means re-appropriating the past—knowing and then living the reality that our Emmanuel is with us in a new way. And it means remembering that God is so much greater than we can ever imagine.

Jesuit priest, paleontologist, biologist, and philosopher Pierre Teilhard de Chardin prayed that he would experience God's infiniteness in the finiteness of the host.

> Lord God, when I go up to your altar for communion, grant that I may derive from it a discernment of the infinite perspective hidden beneath the smallness and closeness of the host in which you are concealed. Already I have accustomed myself to recognize beneath the inertness of the morsel of bread a consuming power that, as the greatest Doctors of your Church have said, far from being absorbed into me, absorbs me into itself. Help me now to overcome that remaining illusion, which would make me think of you as touching me only in a limited and momentary way.
>
> I begin to understand: under the sacramental species you touch me first of all through the "accidents" of matter, of the material bread; but then, in consequence of this, you touch me also through the entire universe inasmuch as the entire universe, thanks to that primary influence,

ebbs and flows over me. In a true sense the arms and the heart, which you open to me, are nothing less than all the united powers of the world, which, permeated through and through by your will, your inclinations, your temperament, bend over my being to form it and feed it and draw it into the blazing center of your infinite fire. In the host, Lord Jesus, you offer me my life.

TRUE REMEMBERING

To truly remember, it is not enough to bring the past to mind. Teilhard's prayer shows that true remembering is really re-membering. That is allowing, with God's guidance, the pieces or members of the past, to be transformed into something new. As our understanding of the past is re-membered, we benefit from it more fully in the present. Another Jesuit, Canadian John English, coined the term "graced history." When we look back and realize that God was present in our past, we experience our history as graced. As our faith deepens, we see God's presence more clearly in both our present and our past.

REMEMBERING WHO WE ARE

The eucharist is built on the four-part action of blessing, breaking, sharing, and eating. We remember who God is and also who we are—God's beloved, made in the divine likeness, set here as stewards of the earth. Through all the scripture stories from before and after Jesus' time on earth, we may remember how we are, at various times, broken and whole, cowardly and courageous, sinners and saints, faithful and disloyal. As we read about those women and men from the past whom God supported, consoled, encouraged, and challenged, we receive the confidence to look for the divine presence active in our own lives.

This gift of remembering who we are, with all our gifts and challenges, is not reserved to any one moment of the eucharistic celebration but is accessible throughout its entirety. As she received communion, Donna Hert was guided to remember.

There is nothing for me that can come close to replicating the experience of meeting Jesus in the eucharist. I attend eucharist as often as I can, and no matter how scattered I am, there is always that moment of seeing the uplifted host and chalice when I am transported spiritually to a place of deep peace and joy that is very real.

In the formative years of early elementary school, I was taught to say (today I would use the word "pray") "My Lord and My God" upon seeing the host lifted up at the consecration. At the consecration of the chalice I was taught to say, "My Lord and My God, tell me what to do and give me the grace to do it." Certainly for many years I was just saying this because I had been told to do so. Over time, however, I grew into an understanding of what I was saying, and now I am overwhelmed by the prayerful truth of those words. It has become a term of endearment for me, very intimate and heartfelt. It also encourages me to be receptive to God's guidance whenever and wherever it is offered.

Of the many poignant experiences I have had during eucharist, I want to share one about God's guidance that I think a number of parents could relate to. It occurred when our son, Stuart, was about eight years old. He was a challenging child in some ways, and one Sunday morning I had had it with him. It had been a trying and difficult time with this child, and, even at church that morning, I was feeling at my wit's end.

Stuart was standing just in front of me in the communion line. As we moved forward, I found myself looking at the back of his head and the white shirt he was wearing. At that moment he looked like such an angel.

As the eucharistic minister held up the host in front of my son, I focused on that host and simply said to Jesus, in desperation, "Do something!" Stuart merrily tromped back to his seat while I received from the cup. When I turned around to go to my seat there was what seemed to be a single shaft of sunlight coming through the nearby window and shining only on Stuart so that he was glowing! I know Jesus was saying to me, "I am doing something. I just came face to face with this beloved child."

From that time on, when I was stressed in my relationship with Stuart, I remembered that experience during Eucharist. I remembered that God was working powerfully in both our lives. I remembered to let God be in control. This memory helped me trust in the efficacy of the eucharist. I was able to be more spiritually detached in a healthy way. It was far from smooth sailing with that child, but I am grateful for the power of Jesus through the eucharist in helping to shape the wonderful young man he is today.

REMEMBERING MORE EFFECTIVELY

Remembering effectively is important for a number of reasons. Firstly, remembering allows us to learn from our past experiences. We may be able to prevent some unwanted things from happening, if we remember similar situations. From Caitlin we have this story.

We were always late for Mass. With three young kids, there was always some crisis that occurred just as we were leaving the house. There just wasn't time to wake everyone, get them dressed and fed and in the car. We usually arrived during the first reading, and I mostly felt irritable and jittery. Also, I was concerned about the disruption we made coming into the church.

Well, it probably seems obvious to others, but Sunday morning Mass had been a tradition for my whole life. So, I just didn't think of options. One day, during the final blessing, I asked, "Please help me, Lord, to get to church on time next week." As Fr. Rick completed the blessing, a piece of awareness came into my consciousness. "Go to Saturday evening Mass." I just about laughed out loud. It was something I had never considered.

Long story short, we are all so happy at the 7:00 pm Mass. The kids are a little sleepy, but that just makes them quieter. They go to bed as soon as we get home, and Patrick and I sit and talk about the readings or the homily. This experience helped me remember to bring my problems to God.

Effective memory also aids us in building a knowledge base so that we can link pieces of information together to build a belief system. The Church's three-year cycle of readings in the lectionary helps this process. In the course of a liturgical year, we encounter stories, lamentations, prayers, and hymns of faith from the history of God's Chosen People in the readings from the Old Testament. We also hear the life story of Jesus, the challenges and issues that faced the newborn Christian communities as recounted in the Acts of the Apostles, the letters, and the Book of Revelation in the New Testament. Some passages return every year; others, every third year. Every feast day encourages us to remember not only the focus of the feast, but also our past experiences of it.

My father's name was Frederic, as is mine. He died two years ago, and one of the times I feel closest to him, and to Christ, is during the Memorial Acclamation at Mass. My favorite acclamation is "Let us proclaim the mystery of faith. Christ has died, Christ is risen, Christ will come again." In those few words, I remember how total is God's love for us. And then, when the priest speaks of our loved ones who have gone home to God, I remember my father. A different memory comes each time. It hurt at first. Now I'm very grateful for them.

And, finally, memorizing something—learning it by heart—allows us to transcend it. The flow of the eucharist is mostly unchanging. This can either make for a boring experience, or it can free up our minds so that we can sink into the flow. We do not need to focus so much on what comes next in the liturgy. Therefore, more of our focus can be exquisitely sensitive to our longing for God and for God's presence. For example, we can tune out when we hear the parable of the prodigal son for the fortieth time, or we can open to the message that God wishes us to take from it *this* time—for *this* time will never come again.

CAREFUL PREPARATION AIDS MEMORY

In our busy lives, it is so easy to view the eucharist as one more appointment. We arrive on time but may not really think about it until we are there. Yet, we know that when we are to attend a meeting that is important to us, whether it is a final contract negotiation or a meeting with our child's teacher, preparation makes the encounter more meaningful. Careful preparation can enhance our experience of the eucharist as well. In order to prepare well, we need to first remember.

We are probably aware of only our ability to remember past experiences, when this process either works very well to our delight or relief, or when it does not produce the result we expect to our frustration or embarrassment. However, the human brain actually has three types of memory. "Sensory memory" lasts, at most, a few seconds. It is the awareness we take in from our hearing, seeing, and touching. If these experiences attract our attention, the sensory memory process sends them to our short-term memory. Short-term memory is temporary and limited. If an experience or piece of information seems important to us, it will be sent to our long-term memory, for storage. Our short-term memory is always emptying. So, if something does not go to long-term storage, it is gone forever.

Carefully preparing for eucharist means involving our three types of memory as we focus on the upcoming celebration. We remember that eucharist is a priority in our lives; we remember that our presence at Mass is not as a spectator, but as a participant. Therefore, we ask ourselves, "What do we want to bring to eucharist? What concerns, joys, questions, and thanksgivings?" Spending a few moments thinking about our current situation helps our clarity. Bernadette spent time remembering, prior to Mass, and then God spoke through a friend to remind her that she was getting off the spiritual path.

> As I got ready to leave for church, I did an internal status check, and realized I really didn't want to be at Mass with that one particular person. I didn't like him, and he didn't like me, and really, I thought, there wasn't enough room in the church for both of us. I, of course, was perfect. . . . I mentioned how I felt to a good friend. His reply was a strong reminder: "If there's room for you,

sweetie, there's room for him." I was able to hear God speaking through my friend and allowed my heart to change. It is a message, though, that is easy to forget. The list of those invited to God's table is very inclusive. I need to remember that when I look around and am too quick to judge who belongs, who's "in" and who is "out."

Our careful preparation, our remembering, may also be helpful to others. This young man approached Nancy at a workshop.

My name's Roger, and I have a problem. I just read in the obituaries that a man I know died suddenly of a stroke. George and I were members of the Outdoors Club, and the only contact we had was while hiking with the group. In spite of our infrequent meetings and the forty years difference in our ages, I really cared for him—and I'm grieving. I loved his sense of humor and kindness, and I'll really miss him the next time I'm on a hiking trail. The funeral is next Tuesday, and I've already booked the time off work.

My problem is I want to wear my hiking clothes to the Mass, to honor our relationship and the activity we loved, but I'm worried his loved ones will think I'm being disrespectful not wearing a suit. I don't know any of them, and I'm sure they've never heard of me.

Nancy suggested to Roger that he tell someone in the family, prior to the funeral, his reason for wearing hiking clothes. There is an information grapevine active in every human group—from families to workplaces, religious communities, and sports teams. In each of these groups, there is at least one person, who, if given information, will spread it rapidly. The young man thanked Nancy and left. The next week, she received an e-mail from him.

> I called the church, and they put me on to a family friend who was helping organize things. I told him why I wanted to wear hiking clothes, and he said he would inform the family. Was I ever surprised when I walked into the church! So many people came up to me and said something like, "You must be Roger. George was passionate about the hiking club, and you represent that part of his life. Thank you so much for coming, and thank you for wearing your hiking clothes." So, although I thought I was the only one who would benefit from my apparel, it turned out that many people felt I had enhanced the service.

EUCHARIST AS REMEMBERING

Roger found his experience of eucharist deepened because of his way of remembering George. Teilhard found remembering that God is so much more than a small, white host deepened his experience of eucharist. Donna Hert found the remembrance that Jesus was parenting Stuart with her changed the mother-son relationship very much for the better. Bernadette found that being reminded of divine commandments brought her back to walking in God's ways. Caitlin remembered to bring her problems to God, and Frederic enjoyed memories of his father, and remembered who Christ is for him. Eucharist as remembering is infinite gift.

Closing Prayer

From Psalm 22, with responses by Nancy Reeves

All the ends of the earth shall remember and turn to the Lord;
and all the families of the nations shall worship before him. For dominion belongs to the Lord, and he rules over the nations (vv. 27–28).

God of history, God of the present, God of the future,
May I always remember that all creation and I belong to you.
Help me have true memories of you,
for I know my memory is sometimes distorted and selective.

To him, indeed, shall all who sleep in the earth bow down;
before him shall bow all who go down to the dust, and I shall live for him.
Posterity will serve him; future generations will be told about the Lord,
and proclaim his deliverance to a people yet unborn,
saying that he has done it (vv. 29–31).

Oh, God, help me to share my memories of you,
so that my brothers and sisters will know you.
Help me to speak clearly and truthfully of you

*to the coming generations so that I
can help to bring your kingdom.*

Amen.

Questions to Journal or Discuss

1. How do you prepare for eucharist? Do you want to change this preparation in any way?
2. What part of the eucharist helps you most to remember who God is and what God has done for you?

Spiritual Activity

Using one of the following passages, write yourself into the story:

- Luke 1:49: What has the Almighty done for you?
- Psalm 118:17: What deeds of the Lord would you recount?
- Psalm 30:11–12: How has God transformed your life?

* * *

From Linnea Good: "Psalm 19: Pure Love."
Words and music at www.linneagood.com.

THREE

THANKSGIVING

Not merely one facet of the eucharistic mystery, thanksgiving is its very center. Without it, there is no Mass.
—Lucien Deiss, *It's the Lord's Supper: Eucharist of Christians*, p. 67

In the prayer of praise, the Berakah, *he [Jesus] does not simply thank the Father for the great events of past history, but also for his own "exaltation."*
—Pope Benedict XVI, *Sacramentum Caritatis*, 10

PRAISE AND THANKSGIVING

Our word *eucharist* comes from one of the Greek words used to translate the Hebrew word *berakah*, to bless. The Greek word *eucharistia* means "thanksgiving," while the Greek word *eulogia*, the other word used to translate *berakah*, means, "to praise and say good things about." Both of these words describe different aspects of our relationship with God. *Eulogia*, or praise, refers to the pure praise we offer to God just because God is God; we are beloved creatures; God is creator, source of life itself. We offer thanksgiving, *eucharistia*, for what God has done for us and given to us. The list is as long as the two Testaments, for each book of the Bible recounts to us God's mighty deeds. God has loved us, given us life, rescued us, guided us, supported us, sustained us, challenged us, saved us, rejoiced over us, fed us, forgiven us, and walked with us. Thanksgiving highlights our relationship with God through Jesus Christ.

When we stand before God among God's people, the Mass gives us words to recognize what God has done for us. Prayers such as the "Holy, Holy," with its focus on the holiness and greatness of God, are a good example of eulogia; the eucharistic prayers, which recount God's great deeds, are excellent examples of thanksgiving. At every Mass, the priest and the rest of the assembly engage in the following dialogue:

> The Lord be with you.
> *And also with you.*
> Lift up your hearts.
> *We lift them up to the Lord.*
> Let us give thanks to the Lord our God.
> *It is right to give God thanks and praise.*

In this short story, Bernadette reflects on this dialogue and speaks of taking time prior to arriving at church to remember and give thanks for our graced moments.

"Really," I thought as once again I said those words, "so what am I thankful for?" It's a question that always makes me stop and think. It's so easy to just rattle those words off without thinking of them. So now, whenever I'm on my way to Mass, I review my week or my day, looking for what I'm grateful to God for. It's a wonderful habit to develop because gratitude is our fundamental attitude at eucharist. Gratitude is a great antidote for our world's cynicism and greed. You can't be grateful and cynical at the same time.

In the last chapter, we spoke of the importance of preparing carefully for worship, by remembering our graced history. This remembering usually evokes gratitude in us. Perhaps you have read Antoine de Saint Exupéry's lovely fairy tale, *The Little Prince*. The fox explains, "If you come at just any time, I shall never know at what hour my heart is to be ready to greet you." Preparing for eucharist by becoming conscious of what we are thankful for, like preparing for the encounter with an intimate friend, makes us more receptive to and enhances our experience of eucharist. Standing in gratitude before God helps us experience the divine presence more fully. Terry wrote the following about being grateful at Mass.

You know they tell you to "sleep on it" when you have a problem. Well, that works for me sometimes. What I do more often is take it to Mass. Even if God doesn't tell me what to do about it during the service, I leave feeling refreshed and can usually see my problem with more perspective. When I have a problem, I kneel as soon as I have found a place, and pray, "Thank you,

God, for what you are already doing about my problem. I am willing to receive your guidance." The eucharist is all about gratitude, and I find that expressing thanks brings me closer to God and helps me remember all the other times God has helped me.

Freely Granted

God grants so much to us freely. *Grant* means "to give someone something or allow them to have something, especially as a favor or a privilege." It is so easy for us human beings to take people, things, and God for granted. We expect certain events without really giving them much attention or become bored with the expected. In her book *Prayer*, Sr. Joyce Rupp writes,

> Because the Mass is a celebration filled with formal, rote prayers, they can become boringly familiar with repetition, causing our minds and hearts to flee elsewhere . . . . It takes real effort to be attentive and responsive if we are to experience spiritual union with God through liturgical prayer. Fortunately, there are always times when I am reawakened to the spiritual potency of the eucharist in spite of my unawareness.
>
> One day when I held out my hands to receive communion, there was no more bread. I felt like a little bird with its mouth open, with nothing to be had. I stood and waited for what seemed an eternity until the eucharistic minister returned with the remaining consecrated wafers. As I returned

to my place, gratitude for the gift I had received encompassed me. (*Prayer*, p. 88)

Being human, we will, at times, take the gift of eucharist for granted. After all, we can go almost anywhere in the world, at almost any time, and join with others in the eucharistic celebration. And, in most places, it is not difficult or dangerous to attend Mass. To keep from taking this incredible gift for granted, we need an attitude of gratitude. Then, when we do slip in our thankfulness, we will, like Joyce, have many experiences that bring us back.

MY YOKE IS EASY

At a recent parish mission, Nancy asked at the end of each night if anyone wanted to share a story about the eucharist. On the last evening, a woman came to the front with a sheet of typed notes. "I wanted to be sure I got it down correctly," she said. "I'm so grateful to God." This is her story.

> My name is Denise Robison; I attend St. Mary's parish in Cranbrook, and I am a convert.
>
> One morning I received a call from Rose, a member of our parish who was a eucharistic minister. She explained to me that she would be moving to Calgary soon and that she had been praying for someone to take her place at Rocky Mountain Lodge, a nursing home, where she was one of the leaders of a communion service.
>
> And guess what? It was my name that came to her mind during her prayer. "What?" I think I

said. "Oh Rose, I don't think so. I feel comfortable with the youth, that's where I feel God wants me to be—yeah, definitely with the youth." Very patiently she said, "Okay, but would you at least please pray about it?" I agreed, prayed about it for a couple of days, and when I didn't "hear" anything from God, didn't think about it again. Until . . .

Two weeks later the phone rings, and guess who? Rose. "Hi Denise, your name just won't leave my mind, it's the only name that keeps coming to me to do the communion Service at the lodge. I think that you are the one." "I really don't think so," I said. "Those places smell bad, you know, they drool. Oh, Rose, I really don't think I can do it." Well, she kept talking until I finally agreed that I would give it a try. I'm thinking, okay, maybe I could do a probation period or something until she realizes I wasn't the one to continue.

So I arrive the first time, take a big deep breath (with lip balm under my nose to perhaps cut the smell), and pray like mad, "This isn't really where God wants me. This isn't really where you want me, right Lord?"

Well let me tell you, did the Lord ever have a surprise in store for me. A gift, WOW!!! What a blessing those older people are in my life, and what a blessing they are to our community. They have touched my heart deeply and are to be truly treasured. That was over eight years ago, and I'm still at the Green Home bringing the Lord to these special people. However, this was just a part of God's plan for me. He wasn't finished yet.

Denise pauses here, looking like she is about to cry. She takes a few deep breaths and continues:

> I believe that through this experience God was preparing me to care for my own mother, who was at this time in the early stages of dementia. She would be placed in the nursing home soon. Being eucharistic minister for the other seniors first helped me be there for my mom. I am so thankful to God. I am so very thankful that Rose was persistent and gave me the call—twice. And I'm thankful that I answered.

God's will is always for the highest good of all. God's desire for us is to live freely in love. When we have a sense that God is calling us to a particular path or choice, we may think, as Denise did, that this will not be a good thing for us. Yet, if we remember that Jesus told us, "My yoke is easy and my burden is light" (Mt 11:30), we can respond to the divine call with gratitude, and then explore further how and when and where it is to be accomplished.

Many, if not all, of the other stories in this book involve gratitude to God. As well as the story we have just read, the next two could also easily find a home in the chapter on eucharist as transformation. They were sent by email when we put out the word that we were collecting stories for this book.

> I'm Loretta, a born, baptized, and confirmed Catholic who lost my Christian faith by grade 12, knew only that God must exist when I started university, and was drawn into a bible study through a friend involved in Campus Christian Outreach. I found the studies incredibly frustrating—anyone

could pick out the answers to the questions if they read the scripture verses, but so what? Nothing touched my heart. I continued to go to Mass and receive the eucharist regularly, not really understanding why, because it really meant nothing to me: Jesus could not possibly be man and God . . . if he even ever existed.

Yet I was drawn to apply for a mission trip to Poland at the end of my second year of university and was eventually granted permission to go. It sounds crazy, but I knew without a shadow of a doubt that knowing Jesus personally and living within his Catholic Church was right for the Poles. It just was not for me. It was a six-week mission, and about the third week—like we did every day—we had daily Mass in the small chapel of the convent we were living in. Like every day, I went up and received the eucharist, went back to my spot, knelt down, and was given the gift of faith! Instantaneously! I could believe in Jesus, he was my Lord and savior, he was real!

It did not stop there. I felt a command to stand up, on top of my chair, and proclaim my new faith in Jesus. I resisted for a time, as only about four people out of the more than twenty on the mission even knew I did not believe in Jesus. Finally I did, and I shocked a few people, I can tell you!

This gift of faith, at that time, did not extend to faith in the Catholic Church and its teachings, but over the next few years I grew in faith in the Church and its teachings, as well, until I could assent to all its teachings, even those I still did not understand or quite agree with.

Would it surprise you to know that fourteen years later, I find that receiving the eucharist just once a week is not nearly enough, and that it is what sustained me through many trials and tribulations? I am so grateful to our patient and faithful God.

And Moira King wrote this.

At age twenty-five, a tug by the Holy Spirit caused me to make a major turnaround from the business fast lane to embark on a "Come and See" program with the Sisters of Charity of the Immaculate Conception. My life was being redirected.

Although my time living in religious community was brief, I would come to realize that in his loving patience, God graciously waits for us to get to know him. The time with my religious sisters greatly enhanced my spiritual formation. I looked forward to lauds and vespers and realized how special these morning and evening prayers had become for me. I was grateful that I could quietly "sit at the Father's feet" in love and adoration and then share so intimately in the sacrament of the eucharist.

> *Adoration means entering the depths of our hearts in communion with the Lord, who makes himself bodily present in the eucharist. In the monstrance, he always entrusts himself to us and asks us to be united with his presence, with his risen body.* (Pope Benedict XVI, Address to Roman Clergy, March 2, 2006)

At twenty-nine, I was married and back in the business world, but living life differently. This time, I was consciously continuing the journey of great love and deep understanding that our heavenly Father has for us. This way of being with God helped me through times of adversity as well as times of joy. I give thanks daily for the many blessings that he has bestowed on me and for loving me so much!

Mother Teresa of Calcutta said: "Ask him to grant you the grace of knowing him, the love of loving him, the courage to serve him. Seek him fervently."

I want to keep my focus on Christ and experience daily love and adoration for him. One of my important epiphanies was realizing that it is prayer, the sacrament of the eucharist and eucharistic adoration that provide me with the guidance, courage, strength, and love to serve him and others more fully.

FINDING OUR WAY IN THE DARK

Imagine these scenarios. Your young brother-in-law has been having headaches that are attributed to a disk problem in the neck. The pain intensifies. A CAT scan reveals a massive brain tumor. Subsequent surgery brings the prognosis—three to six months. You are grieving, angry, devastated, and wondering, "Why?"

Your spouse of fifteen years announces that she's leaving. Your whole future crumbles before you. Your hopes, dreams, and plans dissipate in the storm of intense loss and grieving. You are angry, confused, profoundly wounded.

In these kinds of situations, praise and thanksgiving seem almost impossible. Lament, cries of anger to God, pleadings for consolation in pain seem much more appropriate and certainly more natural. But praise? Thanks? For what are we thanking God at such moments of soul-searing pain? How can we praise God in the darkness of life?

First, we thank God just for being God. As one person commented recently, "We praise God in the morning, not for what God has done today (it may turn out to be a perfectly awful day), but just because God is God." We praise God just for being. This is God's first and enduring gift to us.

Second, we thank God for the kind of presence God manifests in our history. God is always faithful. In Jesus, we recognize the fullness of God's gift of self, for Jesus, in his self-giving, joins us in everything we are but our sinfulness. He joins us in our misery, our hopelessness, and our feelings of abandonment. But God never abandoned Jesus, not even to death, the experience that bears the ultimate potential for cutting us off from God. Like the women at the cross, God endured in love death's agony with Jesus and raised him to new life. If our God did not abandon Jesus in the face of death, why would our God abandon us in the face of our own personal hells, whether they are chosen, inherited, or stumbled into? Why would God turn his face from us when we are suffering, anguishing, or devastated? This is the God of mercy and compassion, the God who treasures us more than the lilies of the fields and the birds of the air, the God who carves us in the palm of his hand! As we thank God for this faithfulness throughout history, our faith assures us that God's tenderness will embrace us even in our darkest misery.

When we are in the darkness, it's easy to lose sight of the horizon. Darkness obliterates familiar landmarks and turns our world topsy-turvy; hostility and fear hem us in. Praising and thanking God restores our horizons. Even if pain still dims our sight, gratitude to God, like the first thin light of dawn, restores perspective. Our sense of direction restored, we can walk forward, choosing a way that honors our identity as followers of Christ.

Thanking God also restores our memory. In times of great anguish, we easily forget everything but our pain. Praise and thanksgiving force us to look through our turmoil to see the signs of goodness all around us, which are signs that our God graces us each day with glimmers of the fullness of the kingdom. In remembering, we recognize that we have reason to hope. What God has done in the past, God will do again. Pain is not the final word.

But such praise will not come easily if we have not developed the habit of praise in all seasons. The Roman Catholic tradition marks the beginning and end of each day with the prayer of praise and intercession called the Liturgy of the Hours, or Morning and Evening Prayer. Unchanging elements of these worship services are the Canticle (Song) of Zechariah (Lk 1:67–79), and the Canticle of Mary (Lk 1:46–55), respectively. Praying (or singing) these canticles every day reminds us of God's wondrous deeds, particularly of God's fidelity to the poor and broken. On some mornings or evenings, our sense of identity with the original pray-er may indeed be strong. But on other days these same prayers remind us most powerfully that "the dawn from on high will break upon us, to give light to those who sit in darkness and in the shadow of death, to guide our feet into the way of peace" (Lk 1:78–79). Then hope, newborn or restored, gives us one more reason to sing God's praise.

THE LOOK AND FEEL OF GRATITUDE

How do you experience and show gratitude? Some echo the hymn "How Can I Keep From Singing?" Others turn inward and speak their thanks in silence. Nancy has just finished some research on spirituality for extroverts. A number of them said that they looked forward to the times in the Mass when they engaged with others, sang, or made responses. During these times, it was easier to express gratitude. These extroverts found the more reflective parts of the celebration less meaningful or even boring. On the other hand, some introverts say they try to stay in reflective mode through the whole Mass. They can experience gratitude more fully in this way.

Brain research shows that introverts and extroverts use very different parts of their brains. We believe Jesus was an "omnivert." He could access both internal and external energy, using all parts of his brain. He delighted in large groups of people yet also spent much time alone in introverted prayer. We will always have an introverted or extroverted inclination, and we need to honor these God-given ways of being. Allowing the Holy Spirit to help us open to the unfamiliar energy and become omniverts, however, will assist us to be more like Jesus.

The experience of eucharist can help us here. The Mass is a wonderful flow between extroverted and introverted energy. If we live in that flow with faith and patience, we will learn how to thank God through inner reflection as well as outer engagement.

FROM SAYING "THANK YOU" TO BEING THANK YOU

In our relationship with God, how do we address the very real dilemma that we encounter often in our human relationships? Someone does something utterly wonderful for you, something totally unearned. Our natural response is to say, "What can I do in return? What can I give them to show my thanks?" And so, in response to these wonderful acts of God, we offer ourselves—our lives—as our expression of thanksgiving.

> Sr. Mary Angelica, ninety-nine years old, eagerly anticipated the eightieth anniversary of being a sister. The plans were set for three sisters to celebrate significant anniversaries in the summer. But as her February anniversary date approached, she realized that it was important that she renew her vows on the anniversary of the actual date, eighty years ago, when she made her first profession. And so it was done.
>
> On her special day, Sr. Angelica remembered those eighty years of service to God as a member of her community. She has been a vowed religious longer than the lifetimes of many people. At Mass, during the Preparation of the Gifts, Sr. Angelica, in

love and gratitude, renewed her vows with such
clarity that all heard. And, then, she heard God
speak to her; "Thank you, Angelica." She was
overwhelmed! God was grateful to her for her
"yes." After the eucharistic celebration, a glowing
Sr. Angelica, not able to contain her joy, shared
with one of her sisters her totally unexpected
response from the God of love.

At the Mass of the Lord's Supper on Holy Thursday, we pray Psalm 116.

> What shall I return to the Lord
> for all his bounty to me?
> I will offer to you a thanksgiving sacrifice
> and call on the name of the Lord.
> I will pay my vows to the Lord in the
> presence of all his people. (vv. 12, 17, & 18)

This phrase "thanksgiving sacrifice" or "sacrifice
of praise" refers to the only gift we can give to God in
return for all that God has done for us: our very lives.
Some of us give our lives as vowed religious men and
women or as diocesan priests. Most of us do so as
married people; some as single people. Our baptismal
vows, those vows we all hold in common, call each
of us to give his or her life back to God. When we
were baptized, we were joined to Christ, who sur-
rendered himself totally to the Father in response to
all the Father had done for him. Our ultimate act of
thanksgiving, of eucharist, is not words of thanksgiving, but this same self-surrender.

YOU ARE WHAT YOU EAT

In 1993, I attended the World Youth Day gathering in Denver, Colorado, with a number of young people from the former Gravelbourg Diocese. As many of you know, the day before the Papal Mass, the pilgrims hike to the designated field and sleep out under the stars. The night in the foothills of the Rockies was chilly, so some of our pilgrims didn't sleep much. The next day, due to the heat, tiredness, and dehydration, three of our pilgrims fainted. One even had an appendicitis attack.

During the Papal mass, I found myself holding an intravenous bottle for one of our youth in one hand and some shade cover in the other hand. I happened to look up, and I saw a priest distributing communion some distance away. "Hmm," I thought, "I may not be able to receive communion. I need to stay with this young person." But then I realized, "I am *being* eucharist—this is my body and blood given for you." Joy filled my heart! At that point I would have been okay with not receiving communion, but one of the young gentlemen in our group came and took my place. As I walked up to receive communion, I felt gratitude in my heart for the inspiration that had come to me. We are called both to receive and to become eucharist.

—Bernice Daratha, O.S.U.
Regina, Saskatchewan

The transformation that the Spirit works on us in the celebration of eucharist is destined for our everyday, everywhere life. Embraced by Christ during the celebration of Mass—guided, transformed, nourished, healed, and reconciled—we are drawn into his self-surrender of praise and thanksgiving. United with him, we are then sent forth to do and be the same, through our words and actions, for those we encounter on our journey through life. We become Eucharist. We become what we eat: Body and Blood of the Lord, broken and poured out for the life of the world.

Closing Prayer

From Psalm 9, with responses by Nancy Reeves

I will give thanks to the Lord with my whole heart;
I will tell of your wonderful deeds.
I will be glad and exult in you;
I will sing praise to your name, O Most High (vv. 1–2).

I am grateful to you for so many reasons;
I could give thanks to you continually,
and never come to the end, O God.
You have been my support, even before I was born.

The Lord is a stronghold for the oppressed,
a stronghold in times of trouble.
And those who know your name put their trust in you,
for you, O Lord, have not forsaken those who seek you (vv. 9–10).

I give you thanks freely, my God.
May my words and actions always show gratitude
for your wondrous love, faithfulness, compassion, and
guiding hand;
and especially for the gift of Jesus in my life.

Amen.

Questions to Journal and Discuss

1. How do you usually express gratitude? Do you tend to be more extroverted or introverted?
2. What is one of your favorite hymns of gratitude? Think of it or sing it, and explore how it affects you on an emotional, physical, mental, and spiritual dimension.

Spiritual Activity

Read Luke 17:11–19. Move into the story in your imagination, first becoming one of the lepers who did not return to Jesus. What was that experience like? Then, move into the story again, becoming the leper who did return, and explore that experience.

Afterward, compare the two.

* * *

From Linnea Good: "Psalm 95: Stand On the Rock and Shout!" Words and music at www.linneagood.com.

FOUR

RECONCILIATION

*Free from sin and alive for God through the Eucharist,
we daily become more fully children of God. The God of
creation re-creates in us the divine life, which was full in
Jesus. Repairing and renewing human nature, building
upon it, grace matures us after the example of the perfect
man, Jesus. We do not become fully Christian on our own,
but by the grace of God. The Risen Lord, who becomes our
Bread of Life, makes our full human potential and our full
Christian development possible.*

—Ernest Falardeau, S.S.S.
One Bread and Cup: Source of Communion, p. 33

*The eucharist is the sacrament of communion between
brothers and sisters who allow themselves to be reconciled
in Christ, who made of Jews and pagans one people, tear-
ing down the wall of hostility that divided them. . . . Only
this constant impulse toward reconciliation enables us to
partake worthily of the body and blood of Christ. . . . In the
memorial of his sacrifice the Lord strengthens our fraternal*

communion and in a particular way urges those in conflict to hasten their reconciliation by opening themselves to dialogue and a commitment to justice.
—Pope Benedict XVI, *Sacramentum Caritatis*, 89

A Radical Oneness in Christ

If we have any awareness beyond our personal experiences, we recognize that our world is wracked by hostilities of all kinds: between nations and races, within families and neighborhoods, and even between and within our churches. Yet, when we ponder the mystery of the eucharist, we recognize that the only fracturing, the only breaking that happens is to the eucharistic bread, the body of Christ. Otherwise it's all about a radical oneness in Christ. We all share the one bread at the one table of Christ. We may even sing, "One bread, one body . . . one cup of blessing." But what of that oneness? What about that neighbor, another parishioner, whom we're not speaking to? Does it matter that she's sitting on the other side of the church, and so we don't really have to see each other when we approach the altar to share in holy communion?

Everything about the communion rite screams "union with"—union with God and with one another. We pray the Lord's Prayer, "*Our* Father . . ." not "*my* Father." We share the sign of peace. It's not "Good morning" or "Hey!" but "The Lord's peace be with you." We shake hands or embrace where it is culturally appropriate. We sing together, the song manifesting the unity of our hearts. We walk together, the music uniting our steps into a procession. We stand as all share in holy communion, a common posture that acknowledges that the Spirit is now fashioning us more deeply into Christ's body. We share, we ingest—and are drawn into—the Lord's own body and life. If we are not reconciled with each other, with our neighbors, with our God, we make a lie out of all these gestures.

Many years ago, Bernadette was working in a summer camp in Barbados. She was one of the leaders of the camp for junior high kids, and a priest was the leader of the camp for the older teens. When they all gathered together for eucharist one morning, the priest, after the sign of the cross, looked at the group and announced, "Some of you have been fighting with each other. This eucharist will not continue until you have made peace with each other."

> I was shocked by his boldness: How long will he have to wait, I wondered, for this reconciliation to take place? Would it even happen? Wait he did—twenty long minutes. Then hesitantly, reluctantly, one youth stood, and walked across the room. He didn't meet the other guy's eyes, but stuck out his hand. Slowly, after ten seconds that felt like ten minutes, the other young man took his hand. The process of peacemaking had begun!
>
> Did it finish there? Hardly. But the priest forced the issue: you can't state oneness with your ritual if you aren't prepared to live it with your bodies. He called each of us there to authenticity, to recognize where in our own lives we needed to attend to peacemaking, healing, and reconciliation

in order to eat and drink of the Lord worthily. Only then can we fully become his body, ready to be broken open and to give life to others.

Invitation to Return Home

I was stressed to the max. I was having difficulties with my boss, my mom's Parkinson's was getting worse, and my fifteen year old daughter was pushing at my limits. I'm a Catholic, so even though I just wanted to chill in front of the TV, I went to Mass. I do feel grateful for the sacrifice that Christ made for me, so it's not just attending out of obligation. I didn't expect what God gave me, though.

In thinking about it later, I realized that, over the years, my responses in the eucharist had become rote. I was so familiar with them, I really didn't think of what I was saying. And, even when the responses changed, Sunday to Sunday, like in the Responsorial Psalm, I didn't really concentrate. The response that time was "Turn to the Lord in your need, and you will live." Well, I said it once and waited to say it again. As I glanced at the missalette, my attention was snagged by the sentence, three paragraphs down, "Let the oppressed see it and be glad; you who seek God, let your hearts revive."

I went through a roller coaster of emotions. When I read the word "oppressed," I felt all my problems as a huge weight on my shoulders. Yup, I'm oppressed. Then it was as if my eye was being pulled towards the next line, "you who seek God, let your hearts revive." Then, I felt a huge sense of guilt and loss. I haven't been seeking God. I've been trying to handle all my difficulties myself. I felt a little dizzy with all the emotions swirling inside me.

Then, I sensed a voice, deep inside me. I knew it was God. I heard, "I've been waiting for you to turn to me." With the words, there was this incredible love and joy. I immediately flashed on the parable of the prodigal son. I was being welcomed home!

At that moment, I heard the reader say *my* lines. I repeated them silently along with her. There were two more opportunities to say the response, and I did it with my whole heart. My wife, Janis, looked at me strangely and said, "Bob?" I whispered back, "I'll tell you about it when we get home." Throughout the rest of that Mass, I must have thought, "Thank you, God!" a thousand times.

Bob felt like a large burden had been lifted from him; he had the sense of coming home to God, and he compared his experience to that in the parable of the prodigal son. Bob experienced reconciliation during that eucharist, yet he didn't even know that he had turned away from God. Over and over the scripture readings at each eucharist invite us to become aware of our wrongdoings, to feel remorse, to confess them to God, and to be forgiven, because reconciliation was what the incarnate Jesus was about. And this call to reconciliation is woven throughout the whole eucharistic celebration.

Sometimes we are like Bob, ignorant of our sins. At other times, we come to Mass very aware of our wrongdoings. When we are thus burdened, we are not free—free to worship wholeheartedly, free to walk in God's ways, free to love others, our Divine Lover, and ourselves in a healthy way. So, early in the liturgy, we participate in the Penitential Rite, an opportunity to hold up our wrongdoings in God's merciful presence. This rite only lasts a few moments, so we need to make the most of this time. It is not so much about our sinfulness as about praising God's mercy.

Some people slowly enumerate their sins, which takes the whole time for this part of the Mass. Being human, though, we will be aware of only some of our wrongdoings. God knows them all. So, rather than imagining ourselves standing before a silent Divine Judge, let us be open to a give and take. Since God knows them anyway, briefly acknowledging our sins, and then being silent, with the intent to "help me to know what else is keeping me from freedom" allows God to guide us. But, while we may silently ponder our sinfulness, the presider calls us into another stance: We praise God for mercy, using the ancient Greek words, *Kryie Eleison* . . . "Lord, have mercy!" These words evoke not just a sense of repentance, but also a sense of awe and wonder at God's reconciling, forgiving love. Yet even this is not to be the end of our interaction with God in this rite. Marnie's story illustrates this:

> After attending the Lenten mission where Nancy talked about the importance of being in partnership with God in the Penitential Rite, I decided to let God in. I realized I usually spent the whole

time telling God what I was remorseful about, leaving God no time to speak to me. So, at the eucharist concluding the mission, I briefly shared my sins, and then asked God to show me what else I needed to attend to.

I listened, and although I didn't hear anything at that time, the next day my conscience pricked me more sharply than usual when I used a white lie to avoid a friend's request. This was the impetus I needed to take the assertiveness training course at the local recreation center that I had been waffling about. I knew that lack of assertiveness had gotten me in trouble before, although I thought it wasn't such a big deal. But now, God really took me up on my offer to inform me of my sins. I realized that lying to my friend was not okay. I phoned her back and told her the Spirit had brought me to task about my lying. She was very gracious about it and even said she would come with me to the assertiveness course.

But that's not all. Go back with me to that eucharist. As I was waiting for God to remind me of my sins and feeling remorse for those I brought up, I felt a sweet, tender mercy. God was forgiving me! Of course, I knew in my head God always forgave me, yet I had never felt the direct experience in my heart. I wasn't expecting to feel God's forgiveness, so I guess I wasn't open to it before.

FORGIVENESS AND THE EUCHARIST

We have been focusing on reconciliation from the point of view of ourselves as offenders. Sometimes, though, we have been offended. Reconciliation is still important. Unwillingness to forgive encourages the "expensive emotions" of hatred, resentment, bitterness, and vengeance. We pay a high price for these emotions because they keep us attached to the wrong that was done to us. They take a lot of energy, keep us from healing, and tend to estrange us from others. Who wants to be around a vengeful, bitter person?

When we forgive, we are free to feel anger, to protect ourselves, and to work for justice and peace. We may not want to continue a relationship with the persons who did something to hurt us, and, if so, we can truly let them go. If we do want a relationship with them, we have the energy to work on a healthy one. Even though we may wish to forgive, it is not possible to do so alone. We need God's grace to truly forgive another.

I'm Sharon Ciebin, a Catholic Women's League member, from Coquitlan, B.C. I was adopted as a child, and when I became an adult, I started the search for my birth parents. Social Services sent me four pages of information about my birth family. Reading it, I felt resentment toward my father. My heart broke for my mother as I learned even more than what I had already imagined she went through.

Even though I knew that as a Christian I needed to forgive him, I found I couldn't do so. It took some time for the agency to find my birth parents, and I prayed regularly for my mom during the waiting period, as I had for over forty years. However, I did not pray for my father.

One Father's Day, I was Eucharistic Minister at Our Lady of Fatima Parish. This was eighteen months after I had contacted social services in New Brunswick. Father Scott's homily was about forgiveness, and I suddenly really knew I had to get there with my dad. I believe the Holy Spirit put this sudden urge to forgive in my heart. I asked God to help me forgive him. Then, after communion, I realized that God's grace had softened my heart. I was able to forgive my father and pray for his intentions. I could even thank God for him.

The very next day social services phoned advising me they had found my parents. This started the healing process for my father—who had carried the guilt of giving me up for forty-five years. I also received a lot of healing. And, because of this experience, the healing is spreading out. I now assist young people who are faced with an unplanned pregnancy.

Today, as I write this story, it is Father's Day. Ten years ago today, I forgave my dad.

Sharon's dad accepted her forgiveness and moved toward healing. What if the other person does not accept our forgiveness or refuses to change his or her hurtful ways? That is certainly unfortunate if the other one either continues to feel guilty or lacks remorse.

Just because they remain restricted, though, does not mean we have to. We can experience the freedom of forgiveness even if the other does not. Although God can stir our hearts to forgive at any time during the eucharist, many people say that The Lord's Prayer has provided a wake up call for them. If we are really listening when we say, "Forgive us our trespasses, as we forgive those who trespass against us," we will be motivated to partner with God in bringing about reconciliation.

GOOD GUILT, BAD GUILT

There are two kinds of guilt. We have already mentioned the concept of expensive emotions. Bad guilt is another example of these. Bad guilt continues to grow and fester in us. It results in self-punishment and a refusal to accept God's forgiveness. Some people think this type of guilt is the natural outcome of their sins. Some even refuse to receive communion because they believe they are so dirty or bad inside. Our God does not coerce us into health, but the Holy Spirit will continue to invite the guilt-ridden person to accept forgiveness.

Marco said that God finally got his attention one day as he said the Lamb of God with the rest of the congregation. As he focused on Jesus' sacrifice, the belief that he could not be forgiven suddenly seemed crazy. Marco remembered that Jesus had set him free, yet he was not letting himself be set free. As he asked for God's help to accept forgiveness, he saw in his mind's eye the poster for the Employee Assistance Program at work. He was initially embarrassed to go for counseling, yet uncovering the attitudes and behavior patterns that kept him from accepting God's forgiveness was just what he needed. He knew God was working through the counselor. Marco then found the Rite of Reconciliation truly liberating for the first time in his life.

THE HUNGER FOR RECONCILIATION

In August 1946, two young Sisters of St. Ann, Ida Brasseur and Margaret Cantwell, first set foot on Alaskan soil. They were to minister there for over forty years, bringing the Good News to various communities, mostly in rural Alaska. After Sr. Ida reminisced awhile, Sr. Margaret added this story.

> I remember the ceremony, in the early 1970s, when Archbishop Ryan installed Sr. Ida as eucharistic minister and gave her the ministry that included leading communion services in tiny communities visited only once a month by a priest. He said something to the effect that Sr. Ida was already well known for the wonderful bread she baked and gave to others, including cinnamon rolls and cornbread. Now, he told us, Sr. Ida will be distributing the Bread of Life, the Body of Christ. There was a comment made that her full religious name was Sr. Mary Ida of the Eucharist, chosen for her devotion to Christ present in the eucharistic bread and wine. Then, the Archbishop celebrated Mass, and Sr. Ida served as eucharistic minister. As I received the consecrated host from her hand, I saw she was crying. I was crying, too.

Sr. Ida told the following story about being a eucharistic minister some forty years ago.

A woman came in from a fish camp, specifically to go to confession and attend Mass. That weekend was to have been the priest's monthly visit. She heard the small plane and made the trek into the church. There she found no priest—only two sisters. I could immediately tell how important this opportunity for confession was to her because the fish were running, and normally, no one left camp at that time. The people needed all the fish they could get to survive. It was, therefore, difficult for me to tell her that priest had been called away to a funeral, and there would be a communion service instead of a Mass.

The woman was very distraught. She told me that her heart was burdened, and she had been looking forward to confession. My heart went out to her. I was concerned she would return to the fish camp still feeling great distress. I felt an obligation to do something for her, so I thought, "What would Jesus do with this woman loaded with pain and concerns?" I believe I was then guided to tell her that although I couldn't absolve her, I could listen, if she wanted to talk. Gratefully, she spilled her story. When she finished, I suggested she pray in front of the tabernacle.

She immediately did so, and in fact prayed on her knees, as close as she could get to the tabernacle, for half an hour. As she knelt, I heard her say, "Lord Jesus, Sister says to tell you all my sins." I sat in the back of the church, in case she needed human support, but which was also far enough away to give her privacy with Jesus. I couldn't hear what she said, although she spoke out loud the whole time.

When she had finished, she came back to where I was seated and looked so peaceful. "I'm so happy," she said, touching my sleeve. So was I!

FROM BROKENNESS TO HEALING

Fr. Theodore Dobson shares this story in his book *Say But the Word: How the Lord's Supper Can Transform Your Life*. He explains that he lived in a house with several other priests. One elderly man had a heart condition.

> He and I had had a difficult relationship for most of the time we had been living there. It began when we discovered we were usually on opposing sides of issues. Soon we found it difficult to talk with each other, then to relate with each other, and finally to simply be with each other. (p. 3)

Prior to leaving for a conference, this priest and Fr. Dobson had a particularly angry exchange. At the conference, Fr. Dobson realized how generally stressed he was and asked Jesus during the eucharist to help him with reconciliation. He sensed Christ inviting him to open his heart more fully to others, which he immediately began to do. And felt his burden lift.

> Soon after I came home, I found myself in a pew during a eucharist that this priest was celebrating. As I watched him, my old feelings of animosity toward him began to rise up unbridled. But when this occurred, I decided to look at my feelings of hurt and anger in light of the cross and the meaning of eucharist. I was filled with shame for

myself and my reactions toward him. Struggling against pride, which resisted admitting I was wrong, I offered our relationship to the Lord. . . . I identified the bread with the angry words that had marked our relationship and the wine with the feelings of hurt and anger in my heart, asking forgiveness for all. When the bread and wine became the Body and Blood of Christ, I believed that our relationship, including all of the difficulties in it, were in his heart, and that he would begin to heal it through grace.

Fr. Dobson said that the next time he had contact with the other priest was when they met on a flight of stairs. Due to his heart condition, the other priest was having difficulty climbing them. Fr. Dobson offered his arm. The other man accepted the offer of help. "From that point on we were able to talk with each other again. Through the self-sacrifice that is eucharist, the sacrament of the Lord's Supper, God had worked the miracle of forgiveness in both of us" (p. 4).

Sometimes reconciliation with others takes time. Each eucharist, however, takes us through the complete process from brokenness to wholeness to a new kind of brokenness—that of the body of Christ, if we will allow it. Then we are sent out to be God's instruments of reconciliation.

We spend much of the liturgy acknowledging our sins and begging for forgiveness, but before we leave, we experience communion, the reconciliation of those who have come in need, who have discovered a community of others like them, and who have encountered the God who forgives. In that spirit of communion and reconciliation we go forward from this eucharist to heal the brokenhearted wherever we meet. (Paul Turner, "Reconciliation within the Eucharistic Liturgy," *Ministry & Liturgy* 33/10, pp.12–14)

Closing Prayer

From Psalm 32, with responses by Nancy Reeves

Happy are those whose transgression is forgiven,
whose sin is covered.
Happy are those to whom the Lord imputes no iniquity,
and in whose spirit there is no deceit (vv. 1–2).

Merciful God,
I know others who can admit their wrongdoing.
I see the relief and release they receive.
Help me take responsibility for all my
thoughts, words, and deeds.

While I kept silence, my body wasted away
through my groaning all day long.
For day and night your hand was heavy upon me;
my strength was dried up as by the heat of summer
(vv. 3–4).

All that happens when I attempt
to hide my wrongs from you
is that I hurt myself with guilt and shame
and other self-punishments.
I even think you are rejecting me.

Then I acknowledged my sin to you,
and I did not hide my iniquity;
I said, "I will confess my transgressions to the Lord."
And you forgave the guilt of my sin (v. 5).

Finally admitting my wrongs to you
I stand in your presence with fear and trembling
only to sense your immediate response,
"Welcome home, my beloved, you are forgiven."

Therefore, let all who are faithful offer prayer to you;
at a time of distress, the rush of mighty waters shall not reach them.
You are a hiding place for me; you preserve me from trouble;
you surround me with glad cries of deliverance (vv. 6–7).
Amen.

Questions to Journal and Discuss

1. Describe a time you experienced reconciliation during the eucharist when you knew you had done something wrong. At what part of the Mass did the reconciliation come?

2. What does it feel like to be forgiven by God? By another person?

Spiritual Activity

Imagine yourself and a group of other people at table with Jesus. You are sitting on his left. Make the scene live as much as possible. Watch him as he blesses and breaks the bread. Then he turns and hands it to you. Spend a little time with this image. Watch him as he hands you the bread, then focus on how you feel. Eat a piece slowly.

Then turn to your left to pass the bread to the next person. For the first time, you realize the person sitting beside you is one with whom you feel estranged. Give the person a piece of bread and then hand him or her the plate. Look into his or her eyes as you do so.

Now turn from them, and let the whole scene go. Stay with the after-effects of the activity for a bit. What do you feel? What are you thinking?

* * *

From Linnea Good: "Psalm 32: How Deep the Peace."
Words and music at www.linneagood.com.

FIVE

HEALING

*The eucharist isn't abstract, a theological instruction,
a creed, a moral precept, a philosophy, or even just an
intimate word. It's bodily, an embrace, a kiss, something
shockingly physical, the real presence in a deeper way than
even the old metaphysics imagined. . . . Skin heals when
touched. It's why Jesus gave us the eucharist.*
—Ronald Rolheiser, O.M.I.
"The Eucharist as Touch," *The Prairie Messenger*,
October 13, 2002

In *Sacramentum Caritatis*, Pope Benedict's exhortation
that flowed from the synod on the eucharist, he writes
that in the eucharist, "Jesus draws us into himself."
Think about that for a moment. So often when we
come to Mass, we think of receiving Jesus, which is
indeed a wonderful experience. But the relationship is
two-way: We encounter the risen Jesus in each other,
in the word that he speaks to us, in the gift of his very

self in his body and blood—and in this encounter Jesus, the Risen One, draws us into himself. Imagine that! We—with all our brokenness, all our limitations, and all our wounds—are drawn into Christ. This startling intimacy with the living God bathes us in divine life and love. It draws us into the tender, powerful, healing life of love that is the Trinity. We are held in the love and tenderness of God as surely as a child is held and nurtured in its mother's womb. We are drawn into the healing river of God's love, as the old spiritual calls it.

In this chapter, we will explore the variety of ways that God offers us healing through the gift of the eucharist. Some of the people whose stories you will read attended Mass, specifically hoping for healing. Others were surprised when they encountered divine healing as they participated in the eucharist. The first story is of this latter type, from a young woman who came to Nancy for psychotherapy.

When Claire came out of her three-week-long coma at Victoria General Hospital, she was told that her father had also survived the car accident. Her mother, however, was dead. At first, her injuries took most of her attention, for both her head and her body were broken. Among other injuries, her jaw and left leg were fractured; she had lost vision in her right eye; and she sustained a diffuse head injury. Some of these injuries would heal; others might restrict her forever. This realization sunk in slowly and painfully, leaving Claire no psychological space to come to terms with the death of her mother.

At twenty-four years of age, Claire was living on her own and loving her full-time work with young children. Petite and slim with a shy, sensitive nature, she had good relationships with her parents, her two younger brothers, and her friends. All together, her future had looked bright. It seemed to Claire that her life and her parent's car shattered simultaneously. She couldn't imagine living on her own again, much less working. She was concerned that men would find her physically and/or mentally unattractive.

Then a major impediment to rehabilitation occurred. A common symptom of acquired brain injury is concrete, rigid thinking. Claire told the neuropsychologist that, according to the Roman Catholic Church, no one could accept the reality of a death without attending the funeral Mass. And she had been in a coma during the service for her mother. Therefore, acknowledging her injuries would mean acknowledging her mother's death and, in Claire's mind, go against church teaching. As a result, Claire refused to participate in the treatment plan set out for her. Because of the brain injury, no one could shift Claire in her too-rigid interpretation of Church teaching.

Claire was referred to me for psychotherapy. In our first session, she said, "I just can't get on with life until I accept her death." As we talked, Claire shared her concern that acknowledging her mom's death meant rejecting her faith. She saw no way out of the problem. After a few sessions to build trust and rapport, I asked Claire if she could imagine developing a ritual to help her. The suggestion evoked a strong negative reaction. For Claire, a ritual must be done in church, and she was certain that the Church would not allow another ceremony. She was equally certain that another ritual would deeply upset her dad.

I asked, "If these two concerns did not exist, how would you feel about taking part in a ritual?" Claire responded that she would welcome that. Her homework from that session was to meet with her parish priest and her father to tell them about her problem. The next psychotherapy session saw an excited Claire announcing that both her priest and her dad were very agreeable to the idea of a ritual. "We're going to have a memorial Mass," she said. Claire was bursting with plans and decisions to make, as her priest wanted her to be deeply involved. In fact, Claire said she would be so busy choosing readings, inviting people to the Mass, organizing a reception afterward, and decorating the church, that she didn't have time for psychotherapy!

She continued, "When Father Gene asked me to help with the Mass, I told him my memory was really bad, and I couldn't think clearly because of my brain injury." The wise pastor responded, "I wonder if there is a program you could go to that would help your brain?" "Oh, yes, Father," I said, "the rehab hospital! I'll go back and work really hard so I can do a good job with the Mass!"

It took Claire three months to improve enough to feel ready to undertake the ceremony. Responding to her invitation, forty people attended the memorial Mass, and all came to the reception afterward. When Claire saw me afterward, she said, "I didn't think I was capable of planning this. I mean, anyone who had come out of what I had. . . . Well, it's made me realize that I don't give myself enough credit."

Claire continued her rehabilitation because of the eucharist, with a more positive self-image and self-esteem. A few years later, she sent me a letter telling of her recent graduation from school and new position working with preschoolers with special needs. She heard one of the children tell his mother, "My teacher has only one eye and walks funny like me. I really like her." Claire saw herself as a role model for her young charges. A few years later, I received wedding pictures in the mail, and a few years after that, a picture of a beaming couple with their new baby. Claire's body might limp through life, but her spirit was soaring.

How God Heals

Nancy's workday as a psychologist is full of people with problems. They struggle to deal with bereavement, chronic illness, financial distress, abuse, relationship estrangement, and other losses. We define "loss" as any experience that restricts us—from the concrete losses we have listed to the more nebulous shattering of a dream or expectation. Loss is a part of life, and God is present with love and healing as we grieve the losses that come our way.

Jesus was no stranger to loss:

- As an infant, Jesus was a refugee who was unable to go home because of the threat of death.
- As a child, Jesus was part of a subject people, struggling to make ends meet under crushing burdens of oppression.

- As he began his public ministry, Jesus heard that his colleague and cousin, John the Baptist, had been brutally murdered.
- Throughout his public ministry, Jesus endured hatred, misunderstanding, and suspicion as he taught and healed wounded, grieving people.
- Jesus was betrayed, made to take part in a mockery of a trial, tortured, and crucified as a criminal.

It was when Jesus knew that his betrayal and death were near that he took bread and wine and gave us himself in the eucharist. Grania Radcliffe speaks of how she received healing through the eucharist when she was deeply worried about her sister.

> My love for the eucharist has always been there since early childhood. And I experience the power of the eucharist, very often, for healing. My family is all back in Ireland. Some five years ago my two brothers died within four months of each other, leaving my sister, who had led a very sheltered life, all alone. My sister and brothers had never married. Since they lived together, the deaths of my brothers were in some ways like losing two husbands for my sister. In her grief, she plummeted into a deep depression, and I felt every one of the thousands of miles that separated us.
>
> I did what I could to support my sister but still felt very anxious for her. I knew this anxiety was not useful and would only make my own life more difficult. So, I went to Mass and put my complete trust in the eucharist by placing all my fears and worries into the chalice at the consecration. Slowly, like a time-released medication, I was given an inner source of strength. That is

how I often experience the healing power of God through the eucharist. No bolt of lightning; just an increasing relief. I am very grateful.

Grania speaks of the healing she received as a time-released medication. For her, healing was a relinquishing of her restrictive fears and worries. We describe healing as being given what we need to live, rather than just exist, with the reality of a loss. So, healing for one person might mean courage, for another love, for another forgiveness, or companionship, and so on.

Healing is different from a "cure" or the total erasure of the loss and its effects. Cure in a person with cancer would mean an elimination of all cancer cells. Cure in an estranged relationship would mean a return to the early honeymoon period in the couple's life. Sometimes cure happens, and sometimes it may seem that those who deserve cure don't get it, while those who we believe do not merit it are cured.

I imagine you also know some people who are cured of their illness yet are not healed. Gwen, who has been cancer-free for ten years, remains bitter that she had such a long time of pain and distress, and she stays bitter for the remainder of her days. Frank's partner admits her wrongs, asks for forgiveness, and changes the actions that contributed to the estrangement. Yet Frank remains suspicious and wary, which soon leads to new marital difficulties that he blames on her. Both Gwen and Frank's problems were cured; yet they did not accept healing.

On the other hand, you probably know some people who still have the restriction in their lives, yet they live and love fully. They are often inspirations to those who come into contact with them. The cancer remains, the relationship is still estranged, yet they allow God to gift them with the qualities they need to accept spiritual and emotional healing.

Why cure happens to some and not others is a mystery that will come clear to us after death. Meanwhile, if we pray only for a cure for our restrictions, we are less likely to see the healing God longs for us to have. When we do pray for healing and cure, it helps to remember that we may not know our deepest needs. Fr. Vince Fink, a Franciscan friar from Victoria, said in a recent homily, "So many people attend Mass and ask for the healing they want. They are disappointed when what they have asked for does not occur. God knows us so much better than we know ourselves and always gives us what we need. Our need may be very different from what we want."

HEALING DURING THE EUCHARIST

God is continually offering healing, yet we don't always realize it. The following observations and stories relate to specific parts of the Mass, although we may, of course, sense God's healing touch anywhere and at any time.

THE HEALING POWER OF MUSIC

Music is woven into the very structure of the eucharist, as essential to it as breath is to our bodies.

Music engages our breath, the very breath of the Spirit that sustains us. We breathe in the Spirit's breath and breathe it out as song. Singing can be powerfully healing. God may reach us through the words of the hymn, or we may find that singing out our pain or longing for healing is a great release.

GOD'S VOICE HEALS

Jason, a father of two teenage boys, was in financial difficulties after losing his job due to downsizing in the mill where he had worked for twenty-five years. Although he felt the strong support of his wife, Jason was worried that his two sons wouldn't respect him unless he was working. The Gospel reading for that Sunday was from Matthew. The following lines jumped out at Jason.

> Do not store up for yourselves treasures on earth, where moth and rust consume and where thieves break in and steal; but store up for yourselves treasures in heaven, where neither moth nor rust consumes and where thieves do not break in and steal. For where your treasure is, there your heart will be also. (Mt 6:19–21)

The understanding that the Holy Spirit put in Jason's heart and mind was that his treasure was love, not money. God's love for him did not change due to circumstances such as unemployment, and Jason was being invited to share the treasure of his love with his sons and wife. "My whole attitude about being unemployed changed after hearing that Gospel passage," Jason shared in a workshop. He explained how he accepted the healing guidance of the scripture by sharing his love with his family. Jason listened more to the joys and concerns of his wife and sons and found a number of free activities to do with them.

As Jason expressed his love more often, he found it expanding. He began to volunteer at the local food bank. A few weeks after the eucharist that changed his life, Jason heard one of his sons tell a friend, "Losing your job would make some guys give up. But not my dad! He's helping poor people." Those words brought tears to Jason's eyes. His boy did not see him as a loser! As his love for others expanded, Jason also found his love for himself changed. He grew in self-esteem and thinks that his confident manner was one of the key reasons he was offered a position with another company after only a few job interviews.

When we ask for healing and don't think God has responded, it can be useful to ask the Divine Healer to help us see the gift that we have been offered and to remember that God is passionate about our free will and will never coerce us into spiritual health. The Holy Spirit may strongly urge us to accept the gift and use it, but will never use force.

PRAYING WITH THE CHRIST WHO HEALS

During the Prayer of the Faithful, we can focus on our personal needs for healing, as well as for the healing of other people and situations. Nancy observes, "Even if I am not aware of something within me or within my life that requires healing, I always ask silently for my own healing as well as those of others in my personal world." Fr. Michael J. McKenna makes this request explicit. He says:

> I'm 79 years old and still a full-time hospital chaplain in two seniors' homes in Montreal. I have seen so many examples of healing during the eucharist that I always begin the Prayer of the Faithful with the following prayer. "Heavenly Father, we ask in a very special way that all of us may experience in our bodies and souls and whole personalities the healing love and power of our Lord Jesus Christ, who is always present as we gather for the holy eucharist. Let us pray to the Lord."

As Fr. Michael's words show, healing may be needed on a physical, emotional, mental, or spiritual level. By becoming familiar with a holistic internal assessment, we can more specifically ask for the healing we need. This, of course, is not to inform God, who already knows our needs. By assessing and acknowledging our pain or concerns, it is easier to see the healing God is offering us.

DELIVER US, LORD, FROM ALL ANXIETY

In the Lord's Prayer we pray, "Give us this day our daily bread." Whether we realize it or not, this is a request for healing. That which nourishes us also heals us. If we are truly present to God during this prayer, we are more likely to experience the nourishing balm that God offers.

After we say, "deliver us from evil," the congregation pauses, and the theme of healing is carried on as the priest says, "Deliver us, Lord, from every evil, and grant us peace in our day. In your mercy keep us free from sin and protect us from all anxiety as we wait in joyful hope for the coming of our savior, Jesus Christ."

Let's focus on that word "anxiety" in the above quote. Many people view fear and anxiety as the same experience, yet there is a big difference between the two. Fear is a healthy response to danger. Our systems receive a shot of adrenaline, and we focus intently on the threat. Assessment comes in a split second, and we run, freeze, or fight, as is most needful. Later, when the danger is past, we may think of or talk about our scary event and find ourselves re-experiencing some of the same symptoms, such as rapid heart rate or sweaty palms. It seems we are afraid, yet there is no threat in our immediate vicinity. What we are experiencing in this later event is anxiety.

Fear is helpful because it focuses our full attention on danger. Initially, anxiety is also helpful. By remembering danger, we are more likely to determine ways to protect ourselves from it in the future. Ongoing anxiety, however, is not helpful. It keeps us in a state of unhealthy arousal. Some common reactions to ongoing anxiety are withdrawal from others, including God; sleep disturbance and nightmares; tendency to startle easily; irritability; and poor concentration. We wonder who was led by God to include that wonderful phrase in the Communion Rite, "protect us from all anxiety."

A young woman approached Nancy on the second night of a Lenten mission on the eucharist. She had tears on her cheeks as she told her story.

> I just want to let you know that I have had an anxiety disorder for five years. Although I'm making some progress with medication and counseling, I haven't been able to stay in a room for more than about twenty minutes. So, during Mass, I leave for a short time, at least once. Even though I know in my head that I'm not going to die, when the anxiety hits, it feels like I am, and I just can't stay.
>
> Well, tonight, I expected to leave half way through, since the mission is an hour and a half. But then you talked about anxiety. A few minutes later, the anxiety surged, and I prayed, "Lord, protect me from all anxiety!" And my anxiety diminished enough for me to stay through the whole evening! I'm so grateful to God.

SKIN HEALS

The experience of peace is often one of the top needs of burdened people. The Sign of Peace at Mass is our opportunity to be an instrument of Christ's peace as we give solace to another. It is also a time we can embrace how Christ uses others to give us peace. In this simple gesture, we can be Christ's skin to each other. Burt thought healing was impossible, but through the Sign of Peace, he began to see otherwise.

I was full of despair after my wife died. No one and nothing could help me to feel better, even though many tried. Some months later, I attended Mass. I had been going regularly, but in my pain, I was just going through the motions. This time, as I shook hand after hand during the passing of Christ's peace, I started to feel a deep sense of peace myself, and the knot of despair inside me began to loosen. I knew God was with me. This was the beginning of my healing.

Many people tell us that their focus during this part of the eucharist is on service. They give Christ's peace, yet don't consciously receive it. By intentionally focusing on receiving as well, we become aware of divine healing power directed toward us, and realize that we can do nothing without God.

BODY AND BLOOD HEALS

Raya Mackenzie is a Grade 11 student at St. Andrew's High School in Victoria, B.C. For Ms. Sander's religion class, she wrote a short essay titled "Broken."

The eucharistic bread is broken. We, as a church, are broken, broken up into individual members of the Body. And these individuals break, too—emotionally, spiritually, and physically. We are broken. And, yet, in its brokenness, the eucharistic bread gives nourishment and healing. In his death, Christ offers us life. So we, too, with all our faults, with all our breaks, can heal each other.

For me, this is the key aspect of what eucharist means. It is an acknowledgement of our imperfections and the expectation that we can mend. In fact, sometimes to fully understand the miracle of life and the wonder of Christ's sacrifice, we need to be broken first. We need to be broken before we can ever become completely whole.

In my own life, I know I did not recognize the fullness of God's grace until I struggled through some difficult times of sorrow and despair. There were times when I felt as if the world was shattering on me, and there was nothing I could do anymore, nothing to hold on to. But I did find something to grasp in the harder times, and that was eucharist. It was the center that pulled me back to my faith, my family, my grounding. It pulled me into the love of God, the love that was broken and comes to heal. Through eucharist I learned that we come to God with absolutely nothing, and he gives freely. In my hard times, sometimes I still left Mass broken. Sometimes, I was not as healed as I wanted to be. But each time, just a little more, I found my wounds closing. I became more whole.

Every time I go to Mass now, I am reminded that I was broken and that I was healed and that I may very well be broken again. But that has little bearing in the miraculous gift of love that God provides if we are willing to help him heal our wounds!

Share the Healing You Have Received

In the Concluding Rite, we receive God's blessing. This is a time to hold up any concern or restriction we have so that as we are dismissed in the peace of Christ to continue to partner with God, we can bring healing to others.

Closing Prayer

From Psalm 145, with responses by Nancy Reeves

All your works shall give thanks to you, O Lord, and all your faithful shall bless you.
They shall speak of the glory of your kingdom and tell of your power,
to make known to all people your mighty deeds, and the glorious splendor of your kingdom (vv. 10–12).

I thank you, O God,
for the mighty deeds you have done for me.
Your unconditional love, guidance, healing, and companionship
have sustained me throughout my life.
I wish to live each day knowing I live
In the glorious splendor of your kingdom.

The Lord is faithful in all his words and gracious in all his deeds.

The Lord upholds all who are falling
and raises up all who are bowed down.
The eyes of all look to you,
and you give them their food in due season.
You open your hand,
satisfying the desire of every living thing
(vv. 13b–16).

You know my deepest needs
while I am still unaware.
Thank you for always thinking
of my highest good.
Help me to see the healing that you offer me,
so I may live in healthy relationship
with you and with all your creation.

The Lord is just in all his ways,
and kind in all his doings.
The Lord is near to all who call on him,
to all who call on him in truth.
He fulfills the desire of all who fear him;
he also hears their cry, and saves them (vv. 17–19).

Amen.

Questions to Journal or Discuss

1. Which of the stories in this chapter spoke most to you? Why?
2. During what part of the Mass do you tend to focus on its healing power?
3. Can you share a time when you were healed but not cured? Or cured, yet not healed?

Spiritual Activity

Partnering with God for Healing

Sometimes we realize we have been praying for a cure and have not been open to the way God has sent us healing. Jesus quoted Isaiah when he sorrowed for people who were not open to the words he wished to give them. He said, "For this people's heart has grown dull, and their ears are hard of hearing, and they have shut their eyes; so that they might not look with their eyes, and listen with their ears, and understand with their heart and turn—and I would heal them" (Mt 13:15).

If you feel Jesus is speaking these words to you, you may wish to write yourself a prayer of intent, telling God that you want divine help to do the following:

- change your heart from dull to a brightness that reflects God's presence
- change your ears so they hear God clearly
- change your eyes so that they open to God's presence
- change your whole being so that you turn more fully in the ways that God wishes you to go and perceive the healing God offers you

Bring your prayer to Mass. You may want to pray it just after you take your seat in the church, during the moment of private confession, silently during the Prayer of the Faithful, or at any other time the Holy Spirit brings it to your mind.

* * *

From Linnea Good: "Psalm 86: O God We Call."
Words and music at www.linneagood.com.

six

NOURISHMENT

The Mass is the spiritual food that sustains me—without which I could not get through one single day or hour in my life.

—Mother Teresa of Calcutta

Our communities, when they celebrate the eucharist, must become ever more conscious that the sacrifice of Christ is for all, and that the eucharist thus compels all who believe in him to become "bread that is broken" for others, and to work for the building of a more just and fraternal world. Keeping in mind the multiplication of the loaves and fishes, we need to realize that Christ continues today to exhort his disciples to become personally engaged: "You yourselves, give them something to eat" (Mt 14:16). Each of us is truly called, together with Jesus, to be bread broken for the life of the world.

—Pope Benedict XVI, *Sacramentum Caritatis*, 88

FOOD AND DRINK FOR OUR WORLD

Hunger is a fundamental human experience of people in all times and places. It refers to the need for food to nourish our bodies, and also to the need to be nourished in spirit. Our contemporary world lives a multi-faceted crisis of hunger: the specter of famine in some countries, the epidemic of obesity in others, and the hunger for truth and wholeness in a world in which our hungers are constantly manipulated by the purveyors of consumerism.

Food and feeding people were central to the ministry of Jesus. He seemed always able to hold together the realities of physical hunger and the equally pressing spiritual hungers for meaning, truth, and freedom. The most striking example of this multi-layered approach to food is the Passover meal that he shared with his disciples on the night before he died. Jesus changed the meaning of this celebration and reality of the bread and cup that the he shared with his disciples. When he proclaimed at table, "Take and eat: this is my body. Take and drink: this is my blood," and his disciples then shared the bread and cup of that holy meal, they were united to his death. Like him, they would be broken and become bread to nourish others. Like him, they would be poured out and bring new life to the world. By sharing in his body and blood, they were united to his death and the freedom from sin that it brings. Nothing could come between them and the love of God made visible in Christ Jesus. United to him, they were united to his self-giving, his "sacrifice of praise" in which Jesus poured out his all to God and to us.

Jesus' giving himself as food and drink is a lasting reminder that there is no nourishment without death. To live, we feed on other forms of life. An old joke asks about the difference in a bacon and egg breakfast between the chicken and the pig: the chicken was involved, the pig was committed. Jesus is the food of commitment: he gave his life as nourishment for us. Holy communion is not just a nice ritual in which all our hungers are satisfied. We are called to commitment equal to that of Jesus: to become food and drink for our world.

The Church's eucharistic tradition, from the earliest accounts we have in the writings of St. Paul, insists on the connection between sharing in Christ's body, and feeding the world. Paul lambastes the Corinthians for eating and drinking to their comfort while ignoring the poor who must come late for the meal and find that the rich have left them nothing. Pope Benedict picks up Christ's challenge to his disciples who wondered how to feed the large crowd that was following him: "You give them something to eat." This is not easy, particularly in a world where we are used to consuming to fulfill our needs.

William T. Cavanaugh points out in his trenchant chapter on the eucharist in *Being Consumed: Economics and Christian Desire* that the eucharist changes the dynamic of consumption. We who are used to being satiated are, in fact, consumed. The dynamic of the world is turned inside out. Consequently, we who have been drawn into Christ's body by feeding on it must in turn become food. Being fed by the body of

Christ should make us hungry for justice, so hungry that we are willing to give of our very substance (our body and blood that has commingled with Christ's) to make sure that no one, either in our own community or anywhere in the world, goes to bed hungry. At the same time that we work together to meet that challenge, we must also attend to the hungers of the human spirit—for dignity, love, communion, meaning, and a place to call home. Only the living God, who offers the divine self in the sacrament of the eucharist, will appease their hunger.

GIVE US THIS DAY OUR DAILY BREAD

Many people experience God nourishing them through the eucharist. Sixteen-year-old Henri wrote that, of the many symbols within the celebration, the bread and wine as food appeals to him most strongly. His "hunger for truth and forgiveness" is met when he receives Christ's body and blood, which then gives him "the opportunity to become a bit more like Christ himself."

Sallie Latkovich, a Sister of St. Joseph from Florida, writes about how God nourished her through the eucharist.

> My dad had begun to experience some mild dementia while living independently, and it was his decision to move to an independent apartment at a retirement facility. After suffering a heart attack, though, he needed to move to assisted

living. Each move meant less independence for my dad. This was difficult for all of the family.

Dad was still in the acute care hospital when it was time to move the contents out of his apartment and into the assisted-living room. It was a physically and psychologically stressful morning for me. Thankfully, two dear friends helped. That day happened to be November 1, the Feast of All Saints, and we movers took a break and decided to go to the noon Mass to celebrate the holy day.

We were all amazed at the nourishment and strength that eucharist provided us. We were truly refreshed, not only from taking a break from the moving, but from the spiritual energy we were given both in the Liturgy of the Word and while receiving communion. After lunch, we returned to the moving, able to complete our task without feeling the burden that we had borne during the morning.

The words Sr. Sallie linked with nourishment were "strengthen" and "refreshment." *To nourish* means to give us the substances we need in order to exist and to be healthy. So nourishment is both essential in our lives and something that enhances them. Other meanings for *nourish* include to encourage a belief, idea or feeling, or to help something develop. God, as our creator and ground of our being, nourishes us in all these ways, at all times. "Give us today our daily bread," we pray in the Lord's Prayer. Even if we don't ask for it, though, God always offers us the nourishment we need and desire, for God's nourishment is a free gift.

HOLISTIC NOURISHMENT

In a recent letter, Sr. Doreen and the Poor Clare Sisters of Duncan, B.C., wrote the following:

> When we gather to celebrate, there is the realization that we do not make this journey alone. We are called by a Love powerful enough to call the universe into being and vulnerable enough to come into our lives as food for the pilgrimage of life. The nourishment usually associated with the eucharist is spiritual nourishment. Our soul is fed by being united with Christ, through the Word of God, and through the other parts of the Mass, which arouse our faith and show us the right path to walk.

This is not the only type of nourishment that God provides for us, though. God may reach out through different parts of the eucharist to feed our minds with knowledge about our spiritual path, an awareness that helps us live more fully, or a message to guide us. Our minds can be stimulated or calmed at various times in the Mass. Eucharist also touches our emotions. Read what these people say.

> My heart seemed to expand as I took in God's love for me during Mass. Then I was able to go out and share that love with my family and, in fact, everyone else I had contact with over the next few days. This is happening more frequently, and now I think of eucharist as a "love transfusion."

* * *

I was dreading the Christmas season, as it would be the first one without Jim. The first Sunday in Advent, as I shook hands during the Sign of Peace, I felt Christ's peace come into me. I also had the sense that God was saying, "Live peace with me." I had thought I would just ignore Christmas, but when I came home from Mass, I decorated the house with ornaments that were signs of peace to me. I still grieved through Advent and Christmas, yet I also feel God's tender presence filling and feeding me strength and courage.

Last, but certainly not least, are our bodies—the temples in which God resides, the flesh that Jesus took on to show how God desires intimate, unbreakable union with humanity. The flow of the eucharist includes our bodies in a number of ways. We are encouraged to demonstrate our faith, our feelings of praise, thanksgiving, love, and even remorse, through our bodies. We stand, kneel, sit, and walk during the celebration. We use our mouths to sing and to speak our love of God, and to take our Lord's Body and Blood into our body and blood.

Christ's presence may be experienced as a physical sensation. "When I receive communion, I often feel an aliveness, like an electrical tingling, as I swallow," said Kiri. Dave related a time he felt a strong physical sensation of a huge hand on his back.

I even looked around, but no one was touching me. It felt so comforting and warm. I knew it was God. Another time God reached out to me on a physical level was when I was extremely busy and found I couldn't relax enough to sleep well. I would lie for hours thinking over all the stuff I had to do. I was at the point of asking my doctor for sleeping pills when I went to Saturday night Mass. During the Prayer of the Faithful, I prayed, "I'm not handling this busyness well, God. I want to follow your guidance in this." Then, after receiving communion, instead of singing along with the hymn, I knelt and just opened myself to Jesus. Well, I nearly fell asleep! The tiredness grew so much that I asked my wife to drive home. I went to bed immediately, fell asleep, and woke at 9:00 a.m. Although my fatigue wasn't completely gone, I felt better than I had in weeks. My wife and I talked about it, and I realized I had been letting my prayer time slip because I thought I was too busy. I was treating God like a luxury in my life, not an essential. Once I got back to praying regularly, I was able to find more balance in my life.

There Is Only One Eucharist

God offers us nourishment regardless of our attitudes and behaviors. We will receive greater benefit from this nourishment, however, if we actively partner with God. The old adage springs to mind: "You can lead a horse to water, but you can't make him drink." We do our part to drink the living water God offers us by treating eucharist as a true ritual rather than a ritualized behavior.

A true ritual is done only once. It is unrepeatable. And, yet, we may attend eucharist weekly, or even daily. And it is a true ritual. The seeming paradox lies in us, not in the eucharist. If we go to Mass believing we know exactly what to expect—sitting, kneeling, standing, lining up, receiving bread and wine, singing, reading the bulletin, talking with friends, shaking hands with the priest—we may go through the familiar experience only partially attending to what we are doing. Eucharist is then experienced as a ritualized behavior, not as a true ritual. We would still receive benefit from attending and fulfill our obligation. However, we may miss seeing and accepting the other benefits our God longs to give us.

A ritualized behavior is a personal habit that involves a number of actions. Examples are driving a car or putting on clothes. The ritualized behavior might be very helpful to us, but we tend to do it with an expectation of what is going to occur and without being fully present. We often do it the same way each time, without expecting or desiring any changes in the routine. Take dressing for the day as an example. Of course, you need to be somewhat intentional, or you will go to your day's activities in bedroom slippers or walk out into the snow wearing a pair of shorts. So, some of your attention needs to be on your choice of clothes. The majority of your attention, though, may be on what you plan to have for breakfast, or the tasks you need to do that day, or the argument you had with a friend yesterday. This is not necessarily wrong. Habits are useful because our attention is freed up for other things.

It is not helpful, though, if we automatically move into habit mode while undertaking a familiar activity. Habit mode encourages us to keep our awareness in the past or future while acting in the present. When we are in habit mode, we usually have only minimal awareness of our present reality. If we attend Mass in habit mode, we will not be receptive to the living God's presence, inviting us into the transformation we need right at that moment.

We experience eucharist as a true ritual when we keep our awareness fully in the present, knowing that this particular time with God will never come again. A true ritual moves us into an extraordinary time, to a time when we come face to face with Holy Mystery. Although we know the words and actions that will structure the eucharist, we do not know how God will come to us. The eucharist can then be viewed as a date with our Creator. We know we will be with God, without knowing where our Beloved is going to take us.

HOW DO WE MEET JESUS?

How would you expect to meet Christ in the eucharist? Because of past experiences, or due to our personalities, or as a result of some teaching we have had, we may have a favorite part of the Mass, a part that seems more spiritual than other parts or more full of God's presence. Some people seem to just endure the hymns, while others come alive as they sing and feel Christ is with them. Receiving communion is, for many people, where they would expect to meet Christ in the eucharist.

The Church, however, teaches that Christ is present in many ways in the liturgical celebration. Christ is present in the person of the minister, the ordained priest who presides at the eucharistic celebration. Furthermore, "he is present, too, in his Word, for it is he who speaks when the Scriptures are read in the Church." "He is present when the church prays and sings, for he has promised 'Where two or three are gathered together in my name, there am I in the midst of them.'" Of course, he is present in the consecrated elements, in the bread and wine that have been changed into his body and blood by the power of the Holy Spirit (*Constitution on the Sacred Liturgy*, 7). Catholics traditionally have called this "the real presence." Pope Paul VI wrote of this presence: "This presence is called the real presence, not to exclude the other kinds as though they were not real, but because it is real par excellence since it is substantial in the sense that Christ, whole and entire, God and man becomes present" (*Mysterium Fidei*, 39). What a wonderful gift that Christ is available to us in so many ways.

Nourishing Community

Sr. Jane Galvin, F.C.J., tells her story.

A moment at Eucharist imprinted on my heart and mind forever occurred many years ago. I had recently returned to Calgary, Alberta, as a resource staff person at the F.C.J. Christian Life Center. I was excited about this ministry especially, as I had just completed eighteen months of study and further training in the art of Spiritual Companioning. I was eager to try out the new ways of being present to persons—information that I had imbibed at the Institute for Spiritual Leadership in Chicago.

Simultaneously the loss of the close-knit community of friends developed during the time of my studies felt like a great hole in my heart. The experiential form of the transformation process into which we allowed ourselves to be led resulted in the group drawing very close together. We came to realize how deeply we knew each other. After all, we had struggled, cried, laughed, failed, and pulled ourselves together, many times.

On this particular day at the community eucharist in the Center's chapel, I was very aware of my Chicago community, now dispersed around the world, most of whom I would never meet again. In the quiet moments after communion, I wondered if I would ever feel part of a group again. I felt alone and out of sync with those around me who had not had the same experience.

As I sat with these difficult feelings, I slowly became aware of an inner quieting and a strong sense of conviction that seemed to express itself physically in my upper chest. It was so at odds with my current experience that I knew the conviction was God-given. My hunger for others was being fed with God's presence. I knew that God was here in this chapel, and that knowing broadened so that I experienced God in the other people in the room. The awareness that came with this knowing was that all would be well. I would receive the nourishment I need from these people. God would help me with this.

Even though this knowing started in my upper chest and became awareness, it was actually an experience on all levels of my being. And it stayed with me for several days, strengthening and nourishing me until I settled into the Center and community life. The power of its truth has never left me, though the physical experience of it has, as I've been missioned elsewhere in the years since. My worry about having my needs met in new situations is gone. God is nourishing me directly in the eucharist and in many other ways, and God will help me connect with those who will nourish me and be nourished by me.

The stories in this chapter, so far, have focused on God nourishing us. Nourishment given to us does not stop with us, however. Jesus asked Simon Peter, and asks us, "Do you love me?" When we answer, " Yes," Jesus says, "Feed my sheep" (Jn 21:17). Earlier, we read about Dave's realization that when he allowed God to nourish him through spiritual practices, he was more balanced and effective at doing his work.

Paul Bernier wrote in his book *Bread Broken and Shared*:

> If we understand eucharist as the mystery of Christ's continuing ability to feed his people, if we know that his bread is broken to be shared with the needy and the poor, this will form our attitude and lend the dynamism of faith to our efforts. We need a clear ideal of what kind of world we are striving to build, and the ideal we take from the Lord's table is that he has given us brothers and sisters the world over who have a claim on us because we accept the bread broken, in order to be. (p.75)

Frederic Ozanam, the founder of the St. Vincent de Paul Society, knew the importance of regularly drinking Living Water. He said, "The best way to economize time is to lose half an hour each day attending Holy Mass." When we try to live for God, helping others and doing other good works, we are at high risk for burnout. Living for God means using the person that we are and the gifts that we have been given. Yet those are not enough. We need to live not only *for* God, but also *with* God. God's grace will sustain us and guide us to the ministry that is right for us. The tasks God sets before us will be a truly "win-win" situation, for God's call is always healing and growthful for all.

> I'm Dorrie, and I first heard about the need for volunteers at the local federal institution when one of the members of the congregation added a prayer for all who had heard the call to visit those in prison. "What wonderful people," I thought. "I could never do that." I was startled when I sensed a response to my thoughts. God seemed to be sending me a big question mark.
>
> I couldn't imagine God was calling me to volunteer in a prison. I'm not very brave, and I didn't think I could be compassionate to someone who had hurt or killed another person. Over the next few weeks, though, my mind kept returning to the thought of prison ministry. Finally, I made an appointment with the chaplain to find out more. I've been a volunteer for three years now, and I think I get more out of it than the prisoners do. That Mass started a new path for me that has been so unexpected and so wonderful. Saying "yes" to God's call has really deepened my faith. I feel I'm now walking the walk and talking the talk, in a way I never have before.

Throughout history, souls have been nourished and mellowed by simply being in the presence of the eucharistic Christ. They begin to understand how they can become eucharistic people; allowing themselves to be taken by Jesus, blessed, broken, and distributed to others for their nourishment, passing on the gift, the wonder, and the grace of Christ. (Stephen Fitzhenry, O.P. "Qualities of a Contemplative Soul," in *Spiritual Life*, Fall 2006, p. 151)

Closing Prayer

From Psalm 81, with responses by Nancy Reeves

Sing aloud to God our strength;
Shout for joy to the God of Jacob.
Raise a song, sound the tambourine,
The sweet lyre with the harp.
Blow the trumpet at the new moon,
At the full moon, on our festal day (vv. 1–3).

Loving God, when we come to worship in praise and thanksgiving,
We meet your abundance.
Your nourishment gives us much more than we need to survive.

I am the Lord your God,
Who brought you up out of the land of Egypt.
Open your mouth wide and I will fill it (v. 10).

May we be receptive to the many ways you offer us our daily bread.

And as we open our mouths,
may we realize you are giving yourself.

I would feed you with the finest of the wheat,
And with honey from the rock I would satisfy you
(v. 16).

May we use the loving bounty you provide us
to strengthen our own loving;
so that we can partner with you to nourish
all those who hunger and thirst.

Amen.

Questions to Journal or Discuss

1. How have you been nourished during the eucharist? Was it in a spiritual, physical, mental, or emotional dimension? Or in more than one dimension?
2. What does the following scripture passage mean to you? "Jesus said to them, 'My food is to do the will of him who sent me and to complete his work'" (Jn 4:34).

Spiritual Activity

A fundamental principle of Christianity is hospitality. Jesus was an inclusive host. If you were a sinner or a saint, a woman or a man, Jew or Gentile, you were welcome at his table. The dictionary defines "hospitality" as kind and generous treatment of a guest. The urge to be kind and generous to another comes out of a feeling of love. As Jesus taught and showed us, hospitality means offering love to another, even if it leads to restriction or death. "No one has greater love than this, to lay down one's life for one's friends" (Jn 15:13). And Jesus, the loving Host, gave his all for us.

The word "host" means someone who provides hospitality. Host also means the bread that becomes Christ's body during the eucharist. Spend some time being aware of the connection between the host you receive and the host or hostess that you are called to become in Christ's name. You may wish to pray, meditate, journal, or discuss this connection.

* * *

From Linnea Good: "Psalm 81: Honey From the Rock." Words and music at www.linneagood.com.

SEVEN

GUIDANCE

May the Holy eucharist and perfect abandonment to God's will be your heaven on earth.
— Blessed Mother Mary Anne Blondin,
Foundress of the Sisters of St. Ann

Once risen, bearing in his flesh the signs of the passion, [Jesus] can pour out the Spirit upon them, making them sharers in his own mission. The Spirit would then teach the disciples all things and bring to their remembrance all that Christ had said, since it falls to him, as the Spirit of truth, to guide the disciples into all truth.
— Pope Benedict XVI, *Sacramentum Caritatis*, 12

THE ROLE OF THE HOLY SPIRIT

It may not be our first instinct to think of the eucharist and the Holy Spirit together. In fact, Pope Benedict

XVI points out that "we need a renewed awareness of the decisive role played by the Holy Spirit . . . in the deepening understanding of the sacred mysteries" (*Sacramentum Caritatis*, 12). The Holy Spirit acts in every aspect of the eucharist. The Holy Spirit gathers God's people together, forming them into the one body of Christ. The word of God proclaimed in the scriptures becomes a living, active word by the power of the Holy Spirit, who also enables us to respond to God's word, not only in our sung response, but more significantly, in our lives (*Introduction to the Lectionary for Mass*, 4, 6). The Holy Spirit transforms our gifts of bread and wine into the body and blood of Christ: that is perhaps the most familiar aspect of the Holy Spirit's work in the eucharist. Equally important is the Holy Spirit's work of transforming the whole assembly more deeply into the body of Christ as we share in holy communion. Finally, filled with the Spirit, we leave, empowered to be the body of Christ in the world.

Logan was twenty-one when God spoke to him during the first reading at Mass.

> I was sitting beside my girlfriend, and my mind was wandering a little. The first reading was from Exodus and told about the people building a golden calf instead of worshipping God. That got my interest; I thought it would make a good TV drama. Then God got really mad at the people and said to Moses, "I have seen this people, how stiff-necked they are. Now let me alone, so that my wrath may burn hot against them and I may consume them; and of you I will make a great nation."

Wow, when I heard "stiff-necked," my stomach started churning and my heart raced. I realized, "I'm stiff-necked!" My girlfriend was complaining about it the other night, but I told her I was just confident and independent. Now, God seemed to be siding with my girlfriend! I still felt shaken after Mass. I was remembering all the times I got into conflicts at work and with people I cared about because I had to have my own way. It was embarrassing.

That night I asked God to help me not be so stiff-necked. It took months, but I was guided to counseling and helped in a lot of other ways to become more flexible. My girlfriend is much happier. And, actually, I am too.

Many Christian authors have written that God's will for us and our own deepest needs and desires are one and the same thing. They were echoing a statement Jesus made to his followers: "My food is to do the will of him who sent me and to complete his work" (Jn 4:34). Doing the will of God nourished Jesus. And it will nourish us to our core, even if we don't know, as is so often the case, what our deepest needs and desires truly are. How do we know, though, what God's will for us is?

It is not enough to read scripture or to ask, "What would Jesus do?" These decision-making methods rely almost exclusively on us. What we end up doing might be in alignment with God's will, yet we have used primarily our own intelligence, knowledge, or other capacities to make the decision. This is psychological decision-making. Spiritual discernment, on the other hand, is more that just using our own gifts. It is believing that when Jesus told his disciples that he would send an advocate to guide them, he was also talking to us. By expecting and learning to discern the guidance of the Holy Spirit, we partner with God in every decision we make.

God offers us guidance through an infinite number of people, places, and experiences at any time of the day or night. We are more likely to be aware of this divine guidance if we are paying attention. Often, people find they focus on God during Mass more than when they are doing other things and so more readily recall the times God has guided them during the eucharist. Ju Li is one such person.

> I was trying to decide whether or not to apply for a new position at work. The new job was appealing in many ways, but it would mean leaving my coworkers. I had become very close to these people during the five years we had worked together. Everybody was giving me advice, and I just couldn't settle on what to do.
>
> One Sunday, during the announcements, I heard Father Gerry say, "This is the last chance to sign up for the women's retreat being held next month. There are only a few spaces left. See Marian after the service if you have questions." Well, I had heard that announcement the previous three Sundays and thought nothing of it. I don't see myself as a retreat kind of a person. You know, quiet and contemplative.
>
> Anyway, when I heard the announcement, I suddenly felt a strong urge to go. The urge was inside me but didn't seem to be coming from me. "Maybe it's the Holy Spirit," I thought. A deep sense of rightness was added to the urge. "Okay,

God," I said silently, "if you want me to go on the retreat, I will go."

Well, I came back from that retreat feeling refreshed and rested and had a deeper connection to God and the other women in my church family. I also knew that I wanted to apply for that job! I had worked myself into such a state of tension prior to the retreat that I wasn't able to decide clearly. The retreat was just what I needed to get some perspective. And, I never would have done it on my own.

God had guided me in the past, but never like this. Before, I had always felt divine guidance through scripture or a homily. What a surprise that the Spirit would use the announcement time!

How can we be more responsive to God's guidance during the eucharist? Ju Li's experience helped her realize that our divine guide is fully present during all parts of the celebration. If we are inclusively receptive, we will see and hear the messages meant for us. It may be easier to be fully present to scripture than to the announcements, yet we may be missing many opportunities for guidance if we are selectively receptive during any part of the Mass.

Another awareness that can help our listening is to view spiritual discernment as an attitude, not just a method. Many people think of spiritual discernment as something they do. When they say, "I'm going to discern about that," they mean they will use some type of discernment method, such as prayer, in order to listen for God's guidance. Although God does invite us to use particular methods, spiritual discernment is basically an attitude. If we cultivate a mind and heart that say, "I desire to be open to your guidance at all times, O God," then we are less likely to miss the little nudges that the Holy Spirit frequently uses to get our attention.

About ten years ago, God guided Nancy and her friend Judi to a number of decisions that saved a man's life.

> Judi and I met most Saturdays, attending the 5:00 p.m. Mass at St. Andrew's Cathedral. Then we would go to her house, make a meal together, and watch a video or just visit. One evening, the presider was a visiting priest from outside the diocese. There is quite a crowd at this Mass, so Judi and I often didn't wait to shake hands with the priest as we were leaving the church.
>
> This night, however, Judi had a sense that it was important to do so. She said to me, "I don't know why, yet I think it would be good to wait." We got into line, and moved slowly forward. When the priest discovered Judi was a prison chaplain, he said, "I've got a man who says he wants to kill himself, and I don't know resources in Victoria to help him." Judi asked some questions, and in response, the priest said, "Well, I put him in the reconciliation room and will go and talk with him after I finish here." He glanced over his shoulder at the reconciliation room that was just behind him.
>
> At that moment, I felt like someone was pushing me hard right between the shoulders. With the push came an inner voice, "Go!" I immediately took the few steps to the reconciliation room and grabbed the doorknob. As I entered, I heard the

priest's protests, and Judi said, "She's a trauma psychologist, it's okay." I closed the door and saw a very distraught man searching the room. When he noticed me, he spoke agitatedly about his need to kill himself. He said he was looking for something to stab himself with. We talked for about ten minutes, and then Judi joined us. The three of us talked for about twenty more minutes, and then the young man agreed that he would go to the hospital with us.

Throughout this encounter, Judi and I were both listening for God's guidance. She sensed to ask him when he had last eaten, and upon hearing that he had been at least a day without food, she suggested that she go home, fix him a meal, and bring it to the hospital emergency room. I would drive him to the hospital. As we left the reconciliation room, my eye noticed a silver crucifix, about a foot long, and very thin. Its shape was knife-like. It was lying on a small table behind two chairs. If the man had been left alone much longer, he would have found it.

It was a long wait in emergency, yet the man was fed, and we both stayed with him until he was admitted. As we left the hospital, we gave thanks to God for the guidance, and marveled at how one nudge of guidance from the Holy Spirit led to another and how God acted as team leader to engage Judi, the priest, and myself in saving this man's life.

Singing into the Way

Have you ever been divinely guided through song? When we sing, we breathe in deeply—breath that is the gift of God's Spirit inspiring us—and we breathe out song. St. Augustine said that those who sing pray twice. Many people say their hearts open more fully to God as they sing their praise, gratitude, and love. God may invite us to attend to the overall theme of the hymn or a particular word or phrase may seem to jump out at us with deep meaning. Sometimes, the hymn or hymn fragment stays with us, returning to our awareness until we get the message.

Music has a great power to affect our emotions. It can move us into feelings, such as love, compassion, tenderness, remorse, sadness, or longing. Song can arouse our faith. It can calm us and stir us up. Poor Clare Sister Wylie is a musician, and she has received much spiritual guidance through music. The story she told us for this book shows how God can use even one note to guide us.

> I had a problem to solve, and I didn't realize I wasn't in a very good position to sort it out. I was feeling a little out of sorts, and in order to deal effectively with my problem, I needed to be balanced and grounded. As I walked past my guitar, the long knotted cord that ties my habit swung against its strings. A high note sounded. It immediately took my full attention, and in that moment, as I resonated with the note, I felt myself coming into the balance I needed.

So much of God's guidance comes through small nudges, such as Sr. Wylie experienced. The Holy Spirit invites us to turn our attention to something and a meaning, suggestion, or direction becomes more apparent.

THY WILL BE DONE

When Jesus was asked how we should pray, he responded with the Lord's Prayer. Contained in a few short sentences, he gave us a prayer that describes our relationship with our Creator, shows us how to be in right relationship with God and others, and helps us ask for the guidance and healing we need. This prayer is so important to the life of a Christian that we say it during every Mass. It is also said in many prayer groups, and during individual, private prayer times. When we say it, whether individually or in a group, we can know that at that moment, thousands of other people around the world are praying it too.

> Pray then in this way; Our Father in heaven, Hallowed be your name.
> Your kingdom come, your will be done, on earth as it is in heaven.
> Give us this day our daily bread. And forgive us our debts, as we also have forgiven our debtors. And do not bring us to the time of trial, but rescue us from the evil one. (Mt 6:9–13)

Although the translations have changed slightly over the years, Christians still include the meaning of each segment. The Lord's Prayer is a wonderful discernment prayer. In it, we say, "Your will be done," acknowledging our desire and willingness to be obedient to divine guidance. We also align ourselves more closely to God through praise and worship, ask for our daily needs to be met, and acknowledge the necessity to forgive others and be forgiven. Lastly we ask that God intervene any time we are in the presence of evil. This prayer says it all.

A Rose for Clare

I'm Clare, and I want to tell you about the time our family was trying to decide where to go for our vacation. The short list resulted in two choices, both equally positive. One choice, driving to Disneyland, involved excitement and stimulation. The other, renting a cabin on Kalamalka Lake, would be more peaceful and quiet. None of the family, adults or children, had a clear preference for one over the other. Yet, we couldn't do both.

Just before we left for church, I asked God, "Please guide us to the vacation that meets your will." I immediately saw in my mind's eye a tightly closed rosebud, full of potential and mystery. I had the sense that, at some point during Mass, God would unfold the rosebud, and we would know which vacation that was right for us.

When I entered the church, I knelt in my pew and prayed, "Your will be done." Periodically, throughout Mass, I looked at my rosebud to see if there was any change. I thought the scriptures or homily would speak to me, as they so often have, but this time I had no sense that either related to my question. I did, however feel fed by them. During the Sign of Peace, though, I looked at my rosebud and saw it was now partially opened. I thought of the peaceful vacation and with the thought came a sense of rightness. As I shook hand after hand, this feeling grew.

I felt such deep gratitude for God's guidance. As I received communion, I imagined the partially opened rose entering the bread and the wine. And when I said "Amen. So be it," I was agreeing to walk the path God had chosen for us. After Mass, I told my family what I had experienced, and they were all delighted. Eight-year-old Gillian told her friends, "God picked a vacation for us." How wonderful to have such a hands-on Creator!

Clare discovered a personal symbol, a rosebud, representing her concern as she gave it over to God in prayer. The Christian faith in general and the eucharist specifically offer us many symbols. Each of us probably has favorite symbols that touch our hearts and minds, deepening our faith. Yet symbols can lose their potency for us if we take them for granted. How many people wear a crucifix daily without even giving a thought to its meaning? The following are suggestions for retaining the symbols of the Church as vibrant doorways into Mystery.

KNOWLEDGE DEEPENS MEANING

The nature of a symbol means that it will never be fully understood. Yet, we need at least some knowledge of a symbol to help us connect with it. When he was Bishop of Victoria, Raymond Roussin, S.M., was a frequent visitor to William Head Institution, a federal prison. One day, prior to the beginning of Mass, he slowly vested in front of the prisoners and volunteers, explaining the significance of each piece of clothing as he put it on. Everyone was fascinated by the rich symbolism. So, from that day on he continued the practice, and the prisoners enjoyed answering his questions about the vestments and explaining their symbolism to newcomers.

Some of our knowledge of a symbol comes with the symbol itself. Bernadette has often invited groups who are studying the eucharist to enter into it by reflecting on bread and wine. "Tell me all the stories that the bread brings to mind." The stories are as diverse as the people in the group, but inevitably we hear stories of hunger, of hunger satisfied, of celebrations, of childhood smells (it's hard to forget the fragrance of freshly baked bread), of gatherings, of family, and, sometimes, of deprivation and emptiness. One elderly Dutch woman told of her feelings of helplessness during World War II as she fed her children the last crusts of bread she had. And of course, someone always mentions the Bread of Life. Symbols bear the weight of human experience in all its facets and invite us more deeply into it.

SYMBOLS NEED FREEDOM TO CHANGE

If we have had an important spiritual experience with a particular symbol, there may be a tendency to lock in that meaning. It feels good to think of the symbol as having a personal meaning to us. This can be restricting if we won't allow God to speak newness through that symbol or if we ignore or dismiss other symbols in the Mass because we think they are not as holy as our favorite. Every symbol is like an onion: It offers us layers and layers of meaning to uncover. Different circumstances of our lives and different experiences will allow us to discover different meanings. Symbols live because the Holy Spirit speaks through them.

DEVELOPING RELATIONSHIPS WITH SYMBOLS

So that we don't take the symbols of our faith for granted, we need to become intentional about developing relationships with them. The symbols will then touch us on deeper levels of our being. The Christian tradition is rich in symbols. Some date to the time of Jesus; others have grown out of the needs of contemporary society. We may find ourselves more attracted to the old or to the new symbols. Many people say that their faith deepened and their experience or perception of God grew when they allowed themselves to meet, without judgment, a symbol that wouldn't normally attract them.

We can "grow" our spiritual discernment "muscle" by practicing being receptive to God's guidance at all times. The eucharist is a God-given training ground for this. The celebration is rich and full of divine guidance in so many ways.

Closing Prayer

From Psalm 23, with responses by Nancy Reeves

The Lord is my shepherd, I shall not want.
He makes me lie down in green pastures;
he leads me beside still waters;
he restores my soul.
He leads me in right paths
for his name's sake (vv. 1–3).

Like a sheep, sometimes I wander from your ways.
Help me to let myself be shepherded.
When I resist your guidance,
help me to realize that you always want
what's best for me.

Even though I walk through the darkest valley,
I fear no evil,
for you are with me;
your rod and your staff—
they comfort me (v. 4).

When pain, loss, or stress is in my life,
your guidance touches me with comfort.
I am grateful that you are willing to be with me
in my darkest valleys.

You prepare a table before me
in the presence of my enemies;
you anoint my head with oil;
my cup overflows (v. 5).

Your guidance takes the whole picture into account.
You know that when I act out of negativity,
I restrict myself and others.
You invite us all to your eucharist
and encourage us to reconcile our differences.

Surely goodness and mercy shall follow me
all the days of my life,
and I shall dwell in the house of the Lord
my whole life long (v. 6).

Amen.

Questions to Journal or Discuss

1. Remember a decision you made that you feel very good about. Now look for God's guiding presence. Write your story or share it with others.
2. When have you received guidance during the eucharist? Write about or share your stories with others.

Spiritual Activity

During the Last Supper, Jesus offered Simon Peter some guidance. Read John 13:1–10 and listen for the meaning God has for you in this scripture passage.

Let God guide you to a discernment method. Below are two possibilities:

- Read the passage repeatedly until a word or phrase captures your attention. Then hold the word or phrase gently in your mind and heart for some days as you wait for its meaning in your life to unfold.
- Put yourself into the passage in your imagination. You may be yourself, or Peter, or another of Jesus' followers. Make the scene live by bringing in sights, sounds, smells, etc.

* * *

From Linnea Good: "Psalm 91: And When You Call for Me."
Words and music at www.linneagood.com.

EIGHT

EMBRACE

Communion is the to-and-fro of love.
—Jean Vanier, founder of L'Arche Communities

The eucharist draws us into Jesus' act of self-oblation. More than just statically receiving the incarnate Logos, we enter into the very dynamic of his self-giving. Jesus "draws us into himself." By allowing itself to be drawn into the open arms of the Lord, [every celebrating community] achieves insertion into his one and undivided body.
—Pope Benedict XVI, *Sacramentum Caritatis,* 11, 15

The term "embrace" can be either a noun or a verb. An embrace is a loving hug. Embrace as a verb means to enter into an experience or connect with it wholeheartedly, to take up something, such as a way of life or belief, and/or to include something as part of a whole. Eucharist as embrace encompasses all of these meanings. In the eucharist, God holds us lovingly, and we open our spiritual arms in return. Also, for us to receive the most benefit from this sacrament, we need to allow its effects to carry over into our whole lives.

Often, when we think of eucharist, we think of it as a most sacred gift that we are given: the body of Christ. Pope Benedict is quick to dispel that idea, pointing out that "Jesus draws us into himself" (*Sacramentum Caritatis* [*SC*], 11). This reverses our often long-held images of what happens when we share in holy communion. We talk about receiving communion—but in fact, we are also received into holy communion. When we share in the body and blood of Christ, we are drawn into his mystical body and into the life and love of the living God who is three persons in one.

Can you imagine being drawn into the life of God and not being changed? Pope Benedict uses a powerful image for the consequences of this embrace. He calls it "a sort of 'nuclear fission'" (*SC*, 11). This embrace generates energy that transforms us and enables each of us, encounter by encounter, to transform reality. Think of how many people share in holy communion each Sunday around the world. Pope Benedict's vision is very challenging. Drawn into Christ, each of us becomes a bearer of divine light in the world around us. We transfer that light to the next person we meet, who in turn passes it on to the next and so on. God's embrace that we experience in holy communion is the most powerful we can ever know.

In his autobiography, *The Seven Storey Mountain*, Thomas Merton relates how God "wooed" him into an embrace through the eucharist even before he had committed to a particular spiritual path. Merton wrote that for some time he had been experiencing an "impulsion" to go to church. When he focused on the inner urging, he realized it was directing him to a Catholic church. One Sunday morning, the urge became irresistible.

> I will not easily forget how I felt that day. First, there was this sweet, strong, gentle, clean urge in me; this firm, growing interior conviction of what I needed to do. It had a suavity, a simplicity about it that I could not easily account for. And when I gave in to it, it did not exult over me and trample me down in its raging haste to land on its prey, but it carried me forward serenely and with purposeful direction. (p. 206)

Merton canceled his plans to leave New York City and spend the day in the country. Instead, he walked quiet streets until he came to the little Church of Corpus Christi. As he responded to the invitation from God, Merton experienced God's delight. He wrote, "God made it a very beautiful Sunday" (p. 207). Entering the church, Merton was attracted to its architecture and "feel." He enjoyed being with the congregation, who he sensed were praying in a genuine, heart-felt manner. Then, Merton heard just the words he needed to hear in the homily, words that would give him the courage to say "yes" to God and "yes" to a much healthier way of living. But as the time came to receive communion, Merton became overwhelmed and frightened by the mystery and fled the church. As he walked out into the sunshine, the fear left him.

Now I walked leisurely down Broadway in the
sun, and my eyes looked about me at a new
world. I could not understand what it was that
had happened to make me so happy, why I was
so much at peace, so content with life, for I was
not yet used to the clean savor that comes with an
actual grace. . . . All I know is that I walked in a
new world. Even the ugly buildings of Columbia
were transfigured in it, and everywhere was
peace in these streets designed for violence and
noise. (p. 211)

God longed for a deeper relationship with Thomas
Merton, as God does with each of us. And the way
God reaches out to us—through love—is an expression of our Creator's very own nature. Many people
experience divine love as an embrace that we can
encounter anytime and anywhere. In this chapter,
though, we will focus on being lovingly embraced by
our God through the eucharist. St. John Chrysostom,
writing in the fourth century, spoke of Christ's presence in the sacrament. "Jesus, for the burning love He
bore us, wished to unite Himself so closely to us that
we should become one and the same with Him, for
such is the dream of true lovers."

Eucharist was initiated as a love feast. "Having
loved his own who were in the world, he loved them
to the end" (Jn 13:1). Jesus gave himself to us fully
then, and continues to do so now. Each part of the
eucharistic celebration demonstrates God's love for
us. Thomas Merton experienced God's love as the
urge to attend Mass and then felt embraced by the
beauty and appealing nature of the day, the church,
and the congregation. The embrace continued in the

words of the homily that touched him deeply. Merton was left, as we so often are when we feel deeply loved, with the sense that the world is somehow different. We may use phrases such as "seeing through rose-colored glasses" or "walking on air" to describe these experiences. Merton says the buildings around him were "transfigured."

The Feast of the Transfiguration celebrates the time Jesus and a few of his followers climbed a high mountain. He was transfigured, and the disciples saw him glowing radiantly as he spoke with Elijah and Moses. You have probably had the experience of transfiguration because it happens every time we give ourselves fully in loving another. This is the living out of the greatest commandment. This is an experience of eternal life.

> Just then a lawyer stood up to test Jesus. "Teacher," he said, "what must I do to inherit eternal life?" He said to him, "What is written in the law? What do you read there?" He answered, "You shall love the Lord your God with all your heart, and will all your soul, and with all your strength, and with all your mind; and your neighbor as yourself." And he said to him, "You have given the right answer; do this, and you will live." (Lk 10:25–28)

Transfiguration would have been a frequent experience for Jesus. It is less frequent with us, yet God longs for us to have it. Transfiguration usually occurs at peak moments in our lives. We may feel a glow in ourselves, or even see it in others during experiences such as getting married, holding our newborn child, making vows of religious vocation, meeting an old friend after a long time apart, being immersed in deep prayer, and so on. It can be difficult to give ourselves fully in love. Yet if we ask for assistance, the Holy Spirit will guide us to the spiritual refining that will heal our psychological wounds and help our hearts expand.

Bonnie is a good example of this. She found it impossible to love deeply because of prior dysfunctional relationships. God embraced her and then taught her to be more loving in relationships.

> My faith was lukewarm until I received the host one day. As I swallowed, I experienced a knowing in my gut. The words of the knowing were, "You are mine, and I love you." I felt a sensation of huge arms holding me gently. I walked around in a delightful daze for weeks. I became passionate about the eucharist. Instead of attending once a week, I went as much as I could on weekdays. This frequency brought a problem to light, however.
>
> I had great difficulty speaking of God as Father, because my own father had been so abusive. And here I was hearing about Father God at church many times during the week. It had been easier to just ignore the term when my attendance was weekly. It was even difficult for me to experience God as Mother, because my mother had not protected me from my father's abuse. I could open myself more trustingly to the Holy Spirit and to Jesus, but Father/Mother God seemed too threatening.
>
> I told my pastor about my turmoil, my longing to open more fully to this God who was loving me, and my anxiety when God got too close;

since then memories of my past surfaced. Fr. Rick heard me out in a very accepting way. He suggested taking the problem to prayer. He said God would help me resolve this difficulty. The Holy Spirit might suggest counseling, spiritual direction, patience while inner refining went on, or numerous other ways out. He said he was always available to talk with me again and to trust that God had a solution.

I did take my problem to prayer. And each time I heard "Father" at church or said it during the Lord's Prayer, I silently asked for help. Very shortly, I began to sense a tender yet strong feminine energy when I went to Mass. Receiving communion seemed like infant feeding. Slowly, I built trust with God as Mother. After some months, I was surprised one day as I received communion to sense a masculine energy. This energy seemed loving, gentle, and very strong. It took months, but with repeated experiences, I let down my guard and could allow God to touch me as Father or Mother. Major healing!

Since then, I notice that the divine presence in the eucharist is always just what I need. And God has infinite ways of being with us, so our relationship is always expanding. My heart is larger so I can accept more of the love God gives me. This reminds me of the quote by St. Margeurite Bourgeoys, foundress of the Sisters of the Congregation of Notre Dame: "It is only the heart of a lover which penetrates the heart of God." Thanks to God, I do have the heart of a lover now.

LOVE IS A MANY-SPLENDORED THING

In her book *Friendship as Sacrament,* Carmen L. Caltagirone writes,

> The beauty of human intimacy is celebrated, reinforced, and better understood within the context of the eucharist. To receive Christ in the eucharist is to experience the greatest intimacy possible. In the eucharistic sharing we have the privilege of receiving God in such a way that he becomes part of us. (p. 40)

When we think of union with God in this way, it is natural to turn our focus to receiving Christ's body and blood. Kate Chaisiriroj finds that the divine love she experiences during this time also connects her to human love.

> I'm a sixteen-year-old exchange student from Thailand. One of the most important aspects of being Catholic, for me, is receiving eucharist. It means a lot to me. It is also one of the most important things for my family, to go to church every Sunday, no matter now busy our schedules are. Now, studying abroad has separated me from my family. One thing that keeps me in deep touch with my family is receiving holy communion. Besides receiving the eucharist as Christ's body, it always represents the love of my family and friends, even though I'm so far away from them. The eucharist is love, an undefined love, which I believe in. God is a messenger between my family and me, sending love to me everywhere, every time, especially during Sunday Mass.

God does not just love us as we receive communion. All parts of the eucharist invite us to open ourselves more fully to God's embrace. And we may experience various facets of God's love during different parts of the celebration. The Responsorial Psalm may remind us of God's faithful or tender love, the scripture readings may show Jesus' tough love. At times, through the Mass, we may encounter divine love as intimate, strong, vulnerable, merciful, and so on.

One of the most powerful experiences Nancy has had during eucharist was when God said "no" to her.

> I had just started a doctoral program at the University of Alberta in counseling psychology. Prior to being accepted into the program, I had signed a contract to provide a week-long workshop to pastors at the Vancouver School of Theology. Since I specialized in grief and loss as a psychologist, they wanted me to teach them about some of the psychological issues involved in helping dying and grieving adults and children. My co-presenter, Rev. Colin Johnstone, would speak on spiritual issues.
>
> Even though it meant missing a week of classes, the chair of my program graciously allowed me to honor my contract. I thoroughly enjoyed the week, and the participants indicated that they found it rewarding. Spending so much time with people who had consciously committed their lives to God was a new experience for me. I had been raised in a non-churchgoing family, and although I believed in and loved God, I was not used to people who talked about their faith so easily and

so often. In that spiritual environment, I felt like a hungry person surrounded by a banquet.

By mid-week, I wondered if continuing in counseling was a mistake. The psychologists I knew rarely spoke of love, compassion, and grace. I thought that maybe I should switch over to a theological college. I brought the matter up to my co-presenter, who asked if I believed God was calling me to make that change. I had to ask him to explain what he meant; the idea that God spoke to and guided people was a new one. After we talked for some time, I admitted that I had heard no word from God on the subject.

Our workshop ended with eucharist. I was pleased to be able to give God thanks for the fantastic week I had had. The eucharistic ministers were participants, and as I handed the cup back, I suddenly experienced the world as sparkling with intense color. Everything was exquisitely beautiful. I was aware of a deep humming that seemed to have no source. Then, I heard one word. The word was "no." Usually, if someone says "no" to me, I withdraw slightly. Yet this time it was said with so much love, that my whole being yearned toward the speaker. I felt I had been pumped so full of love that if any more was to be given me, I would die. There was no fear with that awareness, however.

After what seemed like an eternity, I became aware that the "no" was about changing my course of studies. Once that realization sunk in, the voice said, "Go back to university. I have given you gifts for all my people." At that point, the love retreated slightly, so I was able to walk. I still felt wrapped in the love as in a hug. As I turned to go back to my seat, I was sure that the experience had taken about an hour and that everyone else had heard the voice. I was surprised to see that no one was looking at me and that the person who had received before me was only a few feet away.

I sat in my seat, throbbing with the love that was still inside me. I was not aware of the rest of the service, although I stood when others stood and sat when they sat. My whole focus was on silently repeating, "Oh, God, yes. Yes. Yes." Knowing that God wanted me to pursue my psychological studies kept me going through difficult or uninteresting courses, such as statistics. The knowledge I gained in my psychology courses allowed me to later teach and write books that combined psychology and spirituality in a way that seems healing and growthful to other seekers.

As we experience God's love in different ways, we may find ourselves responding in different ways. Francis of Assisi's love for God resulted in numerous prayers, songs, and the founding of the Franciscan communities. St. Francis spoke of showing love to God by taking on various roles during Mass and afterward. He said, "We are spouses when the faithful soul is joined by the Holy Spirit to our Lord Jesus Christ. We are brothers to him when we do the will of the Father who is in heaven. We are mothers when we carry Him in our heart and body through a divine love and a pure and sincere conscience and give birth to Him through a holy activity which must shine as an example before others." Lovers enjoy broadening and deepening their relationships by becoming many things to each other. Pope Benedict XVI suggests that this embrace has cosmic consequences, for it is "a process leading ultimately to the transfiguration of the entire world, to the point where God will be all in all" (SC, 11). May we become ever more receptive to God's embrace during the eucharist and ever more willing to be drawn into our Beloved. For as God-lover Mechtild of Magdeburg wrote in the thirteenth century, "God has enough of all good things except one: of communion with humans God can never have enough."

Closing Prayer

From Psalm 63, with responses by Nancy Reeves

O God, you are my God, I seek you,
my soul thirsts for you;
my flesh faints for you,
as in a dry and weary land
where there is no water (v. 1).

I love you, O God, for all you have created
and are creating.
I love you for your words of support and guidance
down through the ages.
Yet this is not enough for me.
I long to deepen our relationship,
to sense your presence more fully.

So I have looked upon you in the sanctuary,
beholding your power and glory.
Because your steadfast love is better than life,

my lips will praise you.
So I will bless you as long as I live;
I will lift up my hands and callon your name
(vv. 2–4).

*I want our relationship to be more than a visit on
Sunday
or a few minutes of prayer each day.
I desire to know your presence each moment,
to receive your love and return it with my whole being,
to make you the center of my life.*

My soul is satisfied as with a rich feast,
and my mouth praises you with joyful lips
when I think of you on my bed,
and meditate on you in the watches of the night;
for you have been my help,
and in the shadow of your wings I sing for joy.
My soul clings to you; your right hand upholds me
(vv. 5–8)

Amen.

Questions to Journal or Discuss

1. Remember and explore a time you experienced God's love for you in the eucharist. What type of love was it: tender, faithful, challenging, provocative, etc.? When did you experience it (e.g., during the Responsorial Psalm or as you received communion)?
2. Remember and explore a time you gave yourself fully in love and were transfigured.

Spiritual activity

Divine Heart of Jesus Meditation

Sr. Catherine McKinley, foundress of the Sisters of Providence of St. Vincent de Paul, and her sisters developed this meditation, which they use monthly. This can be done totally in your imagination or during a time of prayer before the Blessed Sacrament. As with any spiritual practice, the more often you engage in it, the more familiar you become with this aspect of relationship with Christ.

The sisters say to imagine Jesus in the Blessed Sacrament showing you his wounded heart. As you focus on the Sacred Heart of Jesus, ask for the gifts that God wishes you to have. Be receptive to any divine nudges that show you what you can do to accept God's gifts.

* * *

From Linnea Good: "Psalm 22: So While I Live."
Words and music at www.linneagood.com.

ⲛⲓⲛⲉ

COMMUNITY

*At the last supper when Jesus said, "This is my body,"
he probably wasn't talking only about the bread. He was
talking about the community gathered there, about their
love and care, about their being together again. He was
talking about himself, Christ present as teacher, healer, and
leader. He was talking about sharing a meal in solidarity.
He was talking about all the sharing they'd done over the
years, all the words they'd spoken, words of truth, love,
kindness. He was talking about the word, his word and
theirs. He was talking, in short, about his body, the body of
Christ, and he was also talking about the bread.*

—Bill Huebsch,
*Rethinking Sacraments: Holy Moments
in Daily Living*, p. 72

The eucharist is Christ, who gives himself to us and continually builds us up as his body. . . . The eucharist is thus constitutive of the church's being and activity. This is why Christian antiquity used the same words, "corpus Christi," to designate Christ's body born of the Virgin Mary, his eucharistic body, and his ecclesial body. This clear data of the tradition helps us to appreciate the inseparability of Christ and the church.
—Pope Benedict XVI, *Sacramentum Caritatis*, 14–15

ONE BODY, MANY PARTS

When we were baptized, we were incorporated into the body of Christ. That sounds like such an esoteric concept! It's anything but that. Take a moment to look at and feel your body. Think of what you are doing: reading this book, and perhaps listening to music, keeping an ear open for your children's voices, or feeling the breeze wafting through an open window or the warmth of a fireplace. Then make a mental list of all the parts of your body that are engaged in this activity: your eyes, brain, hands, heart and lungs, blood vessels, ears, skin . . . the list is significant! All parts of one body—yours. Now, take that mental image of "one body," and think about the body of Christ, with its many members. We are as close and intimate in Christ as the various senses and parts of our bodies, with their diverse functions, are in us. That's our constant reality, regardless of what we are doing.

We are in Christ, and he, as St. Paul explains, is the head of the body, which is enlivened by his Holy Spirit. If the body of Christ is going to work to its maximum potential, each of us needs to consciously assume our role in this body. All have different roles, but no one is without a part to play in this body. We are joined to each other; to millions of people we don't know, as well as to those few whom we do. Those we like are joined to us, just as are those we dislike. It's an intimate relationship that we cannot escape. What follows is a wonderful story about a particular manifestation of our oneness in the Lord.

> My mother, a faith-filled and very devout woman, was unexpectedly diagnosed with terminal cancer in November 1997. Three short months later, on February 21, she died a peaceful death in our hospital's palliative care unit.
>
> My mom was so deeply loved by her ten children and numerous grandchildren who surrounded her bed the afternoon she died. With us on that day was a wonderful and close friend of the family, Fr. Carlos. Just minutes before my mother's death, we all prayed together, and then Fr. Carlos gave holy communion to my mom. In her very last moments she consumed the body and blood of our Lord. This was an incredible witness to our family of her love for the eucharist. Fr. Carlos could not have given our mother a greater gift. She lived her life in communion with Christ and she died in communion with Christ!
>
> Shockingly, just months later, Fr. Carlos was diagnosed with cancer. Upon hearing this, I immediately called the place where he was staying, and spoke to one of the sisters there. She

said Fr. Carlos was limiting his visitors, and then she told me that he was at the cancer clinic that morning. I told the sister that I was a friend, and I asked if I could go to be with him there.

Because he was not expecting to see me, the nurse advised him that he had a visitor. He allowed me into the examining room, where he was waiting to see the doctor. When I walked in, he sat at the end of the room with his head buried in his hands. He looked up, and smiled gently and sadly. I pulled up a chair in front of him. His first words to me were, " I am sooo sorry that you have to see me like this." My words to him, as I took his hands in mine, were, "Who better to understand than us? You were with us when our mother died . . . now let us be here for you." Fr. Carlos died within that year.

Our family smiles when we think of our mother, our father, and Fr. Carlos playing *Farmer's Rummikub* in heaven—a game that we taught Fr. Carlos during his many family visits with us.

Every time we celebrate eucharist, the priest invokes the power of the Holy Spirit two times, first during the Eucharistic Prayer, before the institution narrative, and then afterward. The first time, he asks that the Spirit "come upon these gifts to make them holy, so that they may become for us the body and blood of our Lord, Jesus Christ" (Eucharistic Prayer II). The second time he prays in these or similar words, "Through the power of your Spirit of love include us now and forever among the members of your Son, whose body and blood we share" (Eucharistic Prayer for Mass for Various Needs and Occasions II). There are two elements here: the working of the Holy Spirit and sharing in the body and blood of Christ. When we share in holy communion, the Spirit draws us more deeply and fully into the body of Christ that is the church. Our communion is not only with and in God, but also with each other. The power of the Spirit draws Christ's body together more intimately and strengthens it for its mission of being bread broken for the life of the world. So our "Amen" to "The Body of Christ" does not just assert our faith in Christ's real presence under the form of bread and wine, but in the whole body of Christ, the Church, and proclaims our willingness to work as one body in the world.

One of Jesus' first acts in his public ministry was to gather around himself a small group of men and women on whom he relied to provide his daily needs of nourishment and accommodation. Jesus encouraged large groups to listen to him, and transformed those individuals into community by asking them to share in a meal together. After healing individuals, Jesus often gave the instruction to return to their communities and tell or show what they had experienced. And the God we worship, although one, is also a community of three persons.

Jesus did tell us to pray alone at times, "but whenever you pray, go into your room and shut the door and pray to your Father who is in secret" (Mt 6:6). We sometimes need that private, alone time with God. Yet, it is in communal worship that our reality as social animals is lived out more fully. Jesus told us, "For where two or three are gathered in my name, I am there among them" (Mt 18:20). The structure of the Mass not only encourages but also, when enacted well, creates community. It is within that communion that Christ is present, in bread and cup and in the worshipping assembly.

Fr. Max Oliva is a Jesuit priest, author, and retreat leader. In his book *God of Many Loves*, he writes of how God guided him during the Eucharist to find community at a time when he was feeling fearful and overwhelmed. Fr. Max is an extrovert and needs to engage other people in order to process feelings and concerns. In 1971, during his Jesuit training, Fr. Max went to Calcutta, India, for three months. His ministry was to work with the Brothers of the Missionaries of Charity in a number of places, including Mother Teresa's Home for Dying Destitutes.

Prior to leaving for India, Fr. Max realized he was feeling anxious when he thought of the severe poverty and illness he would encounter. As he focused on this feeling, he became aware of its source. "My anxiety centered on who would be there that I could talk to about what I would be experiencing. As an extrovert, I knew I would either go crazy or give up and come home early if I did not have people to share with."

On his first day, as Fr. Max began to minister to the dying men in Mother Teresa's Home, he found the experience to be as tragic as he had imagined. During a break on the first day, he began to cry as the dying men's suffering overwhelmed him. Fr. Max was unable to continue, and another volunteer took him back to the house of the Brothers of the Missionaries of Charity. There, Fr. Max met with Brother Andrew, the priest who was General Servant of the Brothers, who supported him while he cried and then suggested he take a few days off to acclimatize to Calcutta before deciding if we wanted to return to work with the dying. Father Max tells the rest of the story.

> During those two days, the fear I had felt before leaving home about not having people to talk to about what I was seeing and experiencing resurfaced. I felt comfortable with Brother Andrew, but he was due to leave Calcutta soon. On the second day, I joined the Brothers at Mass, with Brother Andrew presiding. The gospel reading was the story of the multiplication of the loaves and fishes. In his homily, Brother Andrew commented on the fact that after everyone had eaten, there was still food left over. "What this means to me," he said, "is that God provides not only what we need but more than we need to do his work." This insight jolted me as I realized it contained the answer to my fears. I had to believe God would provide what I needed—people to share with—and even more than I would need to help me process my feelings and thoughts during my time in Calcutta. And that is precisely what did happen. I met people throughout the summer, in various places, who helped me make sense of what I was going through in order to integrate it.

LIVING THE COMMANDMENT

Eucharist invites us to immediately live out the commandment to love God with our whole being and our neighbors as ourselves. We accept this invitation when we come to worship, interested in and willing to communicate with other people as well as with

God. The word "communicate" has a number of meanings: to give or exchange information; to transmit or reveal a feeling or thought; to share a good personal understanding; to be connected or provide access to each other; to administer holy communion; and to receive holy communion. It is possible to communicate in a narrow way by attending Mass focused solely on God. But then we are living only half of the commandment.

Lucie Leduc didn't expect to have a personal connection with God. Her goal in attending church was to find some supportive people. She waited for others to reach out to her and found that didn't happen to the depth that she had hoped. And then, one day, it all changed for her.

> I was in my early twenties and going through a rough time in my life. My marriage was in trouble, and I had two young children. I attended Mass out of duty and because I did feel some sense of belonging with the community. I didn't feel, though, as if I was getting any spiritual comfort out of the experience. I hadn't had any first-hand experience of God, and I often doubted and questioned the religious faith I'd been raised in.
>
> One Sunday, as I was watching people receive communion, I was very suddenly filled with a profound awareness that God loved these people. This insight expanded to include all people, the communion of saints, and me. I knew we were one in God. This knowledge exploded within me into a unitive experience. It left me with a deep sense of safety, security, and of belonging.

I finally knew what eucharist is; what a gift we have been given. It is a welcome to the deepest community—direct relationship with the Holy Trinity and with all of humanity. And, because I could also feel God's love for others, I found I cared about them, too. After that experience, I reached out to other members of the congregation. I found them very responsive, and now I have a number of deep friendships, which have lasted many years. My parish home is a small reflection of my home in God.

Lucie found God and other people in a way she had never expected! God gave her the experience of knowing how loved we are, yet she needed to say "yes" to God's invitation to move more deeply into relationship. If Lucie had continued with her hope that others would reach out to her while she sat waiting, the situation would not have changed. In fact, she could have taken the awareness God gave her and twisted it in her mind to feel even more sorry for herself, thinking, "God loves them, but not me." Lucie, however, was ready to open to God and to others. And acting on her awareness, reaching out rather than waiting, brought her the community she had longed for. Here is another story about reaching out, sent by Jennifer Foley.

During a recent trip to Banff for the National Conference for Catholic Youth Ministers, one of the keynote speakers shared the most powerful witness to faith that he had ever seen. There was a frazzled single mother with five children under the age of eight, sitting in the front pew at Mass, and her baby started to cry. The priest presider came down off the altar to hold the screaming child and continued his homily. This struck me as well-lived faith at the time, and I asked myself why it didn't happen more often.

Each of my sessions, being held in the main conference room, gave me an opportunity to discern how it was going to be possible to overcome challenges and meet goals that our parish is working toward. The entire wall of this room was made up of windows which allowed me to see the top of the mountains but not able to see the ground below. This left a huge space between where we were and the top of the mountain. This gap bothered me for some time, reminding me of where we were as a parish and where we wanted to go. During our last Mass of that gathering, I was powerfully reminded of the obvious answer to my concerns about the parish as the priest lifted the body of Christ, filling the gap. It was a humbling reminder. . . .

A week later, I found myself attending a FacetoFace retreat held in Swift Current, not really knowing why I had been called to be there. When it came to the last Mass, a mother, with two small girls around the ages of two and four, started to have trouble with her youngest. The child started a mix of screaming and crying. It was the most raw, most insistent cry that I have ever heard. Thinking of Banff, I said to myself, "You've got to be kidding me!" The stressed mother packed everything up, leaving her pew just after the gospel, and moved to the back of the church where the young one continued to scream through the homily. Her screams subsided shortly after the homily, allowing her mother to return to her seat, only two pews in front of me.

As people slowly lined up for communion, her raw cry began again. In a community that should be the most caring, compassionate family you could find, I struggled with why no one got up to help her. What I struggled with even more was why *I* didn't and couldn't seem to get up to help her. The mother left for the back of the church, with a look of desperation in her eyes, as the pew before her stood to go receive communion. As I walked to receive Christ that Sunday, all I could hear was the rawness of a crying child. All I could focus on was the look of desperation on the mother's face as she left the pew. All I could think about was how stupid it was that I was going for communion with her struggling at the back of the church.

I received the body and blood of Christ and, without thinking about it or realizing it, walked right past my pew and to the back of the church, where I thanked the now crying mother for coming to church that day, offering to hold her daughter while she went to communion. Her response, "Sometimes it's just so hard. Thank you, but no. I don't want them to see me like this." I stayed for a time, distracting the oldest daughter, who wanted to know why Mommy was crying. Then, when Mom seemed to have gathered herself together, I offered again to no avail. I returned to my pew to pray and knelt down as the music ministry team began to sing "Refiner's Fire." Talk about a powerful reminder that what I couldn't do on my own was powerfully possible when I accepted Christ into the situation. Later, a friend told me that although the mother wasn't able to receive Christ that mass, she did experience the next best thing—the living body of Christ through me.

COMMUNITY DURING EUCHARIST

In his pastoral letter *Living Eucharist: Gathered, Nourished, Sent,* Most Reverend Robert N. Lynch, Bishop of St. Petersburg, writes:

> Unlike a football game, where all the action takes place on the field, the Liturgy of the eucharist invites us, as it were, to come out of the stands and join Christ, the priest, and our brothers and sisters on the playing field. A Sunday Eucharist that is celebrated well involves full, conscious, and active participation, not just passive spectatorship.
>
> The Eucharistic Prayer highlights the communal aspect of the liturgy: "*We* come to you Father . . . *We* ask you to bless and accept these gifts . . . *We* offer them in spirit and in truth." That we worship as a community at Mass cannot be emphasized too strongly. The liturgy is truly "the work of the people" led by the priest and made possible by the power of the Holy Spirit.

In Nancy's research on ritual, she found that an essential element for a true ritual is the presence of others as supporters, witnesses, or includers. Supporters encourage and give solace to us on our journey through life, while witnesses acknowledge the reality of our experiences and speak of their own journey. Includers welcome us into community. Some of the people who participated in Nancy's study said that they had engaged in their healing ritual alone; yet, they asked others to pray for them at a certain time, or they asked others to help them develop their ritual or to debrief with them afterwards.

The eucharistic celebration of today has developed over hundreds of years, as many people experience God present to them in a wide variety of ways. We sometimes encounter God in the parts of the liturgy that invite us to turn inward, to be more introverted as we worship. Other times we find God in the parts that encourage us to worship by interacting with our brothers and sisters. One of these later parts is the Sign of Peace. We will receive the most benefit during this time by being intentionally present to others, as well as to God. Nancy tells the following story that happened to her recently.

> Personally, during the Sign of Peace, I ask who particularly needs Christ's peace at this moment. Well, a few weeks ago, after sharing the Sign of Peace with the folks sitting around me, I asked for God's guidance. As I looked around the church, my attention was 'snagged' by one particular woman across the aisle. I didn't know her and think she may have been new. I walked over to her and held out my hand. She looked a little startled because she and most others had already turned back to the priest, who was now behind the altar. As we were all leaving the church, this woman approached me and said, with a big smile, "Thank you for being so friendly." I said she was welcome, and the woman walked off. I was

puzzled about this encounter until I remembered the Sign of Peace. God has not told me why it was important to go to this woman. Judging from her response, though, my action was meaningful to her.

Another way to be fully present to community in this part of Mass is to realize that Christ's peace is being given to you at the same time as you are an instrument to pass it to others. This may seem obvious, but many people say their focus is on giving or extending the peace. After Nancy spoke of this at a recent Lenten mission, she heard one man say during the concluding eucharist, "And I'm receiving his peace, as well as giving it to you!" The woman, whose hand he held, smiled back and said, "God loves each of us so much."

What we give and receive is not solely Christ's peace. As community, we are also giving and receiving a personal, human peace. This touches sixteen-year-old Frazer Chambers very strongly. He wrote, "Eucharist means togetherness to me. Everybody from school moves together to the church and sits together there as one. The community of the church is a community of communities. The time that best emphasizes this for me is the giving of peace to everyone. This act of giving peace makes everyone feel welcomed and relaxed." And, let us not forget that God and people are not the only ones there during the eucharistic celebration. There is also present a "cloud of witnesses": angels, saints, and ancestors, who are messengers of God's love.

EUCHARIST AFTER EUCHARIST

The word "Mass" (*Missa*) comes from the Latin for dismissal (*Misso*). We are dismissed from our eucharistic celebration to live what we have just celebrated, to live in communion with God and our sisters and brothers. As we are sent out, refreshed, loved, and blessed, this is a time to acknowledge that God is going with us into the world. It is important that we realize that we are not just going out *for* Christ, but *with* Christ. We may share Christ with others in a number of ways. In the following story, Janis Hayden of Chicago speaks of being community within and outside of the eucharistic celebration.

> Eucharist for me is sharing faith, doubt, happiness, sadness, celebrations, death, family, children, health, and illness. I remember one time at Mass sitting next to a woman who was crying. Contrary to popular belief, I am not a person who steps out of my comfort zone often, but I reached over and held her hand for just a moment. It was a moment that I have not forgotten even though it was many years ago. The eucharist made that happen.
>
> Then God called me to be community in a different way. At that time, my mother was in the hospital (where I worked), and every day I would get on the same elevator to go to see her. On that elevator was a sign expressing a need for eucharistic ministers for the sick in that hospital. I successfully ignored it for several days; then I turned my back on it for several more days; and then finally I realized that God was asking me to do this, so I made the call and started the training,

which increased my faith and increased my faith-based friends.

I can remember sometimes walking out of rooms wanting to punch the wall because of the sick and old people who were suffering and dying alone with no family member or someone who cared. They all seemed to find comfort at the sight of me holding the eucharist, but it was very difficult for me to leave them knowing that they would again be alone.

Many years later my uncle, Fr. Sullivan, a diocesan priest, died. My aunt, brother, sisters, and I were greeting people during the wake when a priest came up to me to give condolences. The other people who had spoken to me knew my uncle, but this priest said he had never met him. He came to the wake because many years ago he was given communion by one of Fr. Sullivan's nieces when he was in the hospital. And he was very grateful for the time spent with him when he was sick and needed to talk. That niece was me!

Since that time, I try to remember the impact one person can have on another without knowing it and also the impact that the eucharist has on bringing people together when they most need it; not only the receiver but maybe especially the giver. Being part of the eucharist can happen in more than one way.

We also become eucharist for others and develop faith communities by sharing our faith. Have you found some of the stories in this book inspiring? Have you ever been inspired by words spoken through other writers or speakers? A prophet is one who speaks by divine inspiration. Although the ministry of professional prophecy is only given to some, I believe God invites each of us to share the Good News. As we say "yes" to being lay prophets, the Holy Spirit will help us with the logistics.

Often, lay prophets share the Good News by being the hands and feet of Christ. As St. Francis said, "Preach the Gospel at all times, and when necessary use words." It is through our loving and faithful actions that others are inspired. A friend of mine told me of an incident at work when a co-worker asked her, "How could you be nice to that customer? She's so obnoxious! You set your limits without yelling at her. I would have lost it. " My friend replied, "It was difficult, yet my faith has helped me grow in calmness and compassion." Nothing more was said for a few weeks. Then the co-worker returned to the subject. "I've been watching you since that obnoxious woman was in. Could you tell me a little more about your beliefs? I think I need a faith to help me through right now."

Another way to be a lay prophet is to tell the stories of our own faith journey. This is often more difficult than just speaking with others about Christian beliefs, scripture, or the story of Jesus Christ. It can feel vulnerable to share our own experiences with God. Or we may worry others won't believe us or will think we are religious fanatics. Sharing our own spiritual experiences, though, may help others hear the Good News more effectively than those other methods.

Almost everyone you meet will have learned something about Christianity. Some will be nominal Christians. Telling them more about what they already know is not likely to pique their interest. Sharing an experience you yourself have had shows them that God is vitally present in the lives of ordinary people. Your own story will hold a deep truth for them. When we speak of sharing our God touches, we're not suggesting walking up to strangers and telling them your most intimate experiences. Instead, we advocate being receptive to opportunities for gentle faith sharing. Sharing our own faith experiences is much less threatening to people who have had someone's form of Christianity rammed down their throats.

Sharing our experiences of eucharist may be helpful to non-church-goers or people of other faith traditions. Also, it is very helpful for other Christians, particularly those in our own congregation or family, to hear of our God touches. So often, after Mass, we hear folks talking about their grandchildren or gardens. This type of sharing is important to build community, yet it is not enough to build a faith community. How inspiring it is if someone also speaks of how God came to them during the service, with words such as "During the First Reading, I sensed God directing me to a particular line. I'm not sure what it means yet, but I think it's about the problem I'm having at work. I feel more settled already. God is with me on this."

COMMUNITY OF BELIEVERS

"There is strength in numbers," says the old adage. We hope that some of the stories and concepts in this chapter will deepen your experience of eucharist as community. Then the fretting baby, the coughing woman, the person that sings off-key into your ear, and the elderly priest who sometimes forgets where he is in the Mass will be for you examples of how God loves us and gathers us in, whoever we are, however we are. We hope that with this awareness, your presence as part of this community will continually strengthen and deepen your experience of the eucharist.

Closing Prayer

From Psalm 96:1–9, with responses by Nancy Reeves

O sing to the Lord a new song;
sing to the Lord, all the earth.
Sing to the Lord, bless his name;
tell of his salvation from day to day.
Declare his glory among the nations,
His marvelous works among all the peoples.
For great is the Lord, and greatly to be praised;
he is to be revered above all gods (vv. 1–4).

We truly know we are part of the body of Christ
when we worship together.
May my presence at the eucharist
strengthen the love I have for you, my God,
as well as my love for my sisters and brothers.

Ascribe to the Lord, O families of the peoples,
ascribe to the Lord glory and strength.
Ascribe to the Lord the glory due his name;
bring an offering, and come into his courts.

Worship the Lord in holy splendor;
tremble before him, all the earth (vv. 5–9).

We come as community to meet in communion,
with the community of the Holy Trinity.
Jesus prayed that we may all be one.
We pray this too, in the name of the Father,
and of the Son, and of the Holy Spirit.

Amen.

Questions to Journal or Discuss

1. What part of the eucharist speaks most clearly to
   you of community?
2. Have you had an experience when another person
   showed care and concern for you during the eucharist? If so, describe it.

Spiritual Activity

Sit or lie comfortably and close your eyes. Take a
trip in your imagination, seeing or thinking about
your own faith community celebrating eucharist
together, and then broaden your view. If you have
worshipped with other communities, bring them to
mind. Remember scenes of eucharist in other countries that you have seen on television or as pictures
in magazines. Then imagine people in other countries
during their eucharistic celebrations.

Now, imagine or see all of these faith communities
being united in God's love. Then imagine you as

part of this whole. Be with this experience for a time, allowing God to send love through you, as well as allowing yourself to receive divine love through this worldwide prayer and act of worship.

* * *

From Linnea Good: "Psalm 122: I Rejoiced."
Words and music at www.linneagood.com.

TEN

CELEBRATION

This sacrament was instituted to confer on us not merely particular graces, but all the gifts of the life of the incarnate God as well.

—John A. Kane
Transforming Your Life Through the Eucharist, p. 90

Celebrations are gatherings, usually involving a number of people. They are associated with happiness and rejoicing. To celebrate something is to mark it as special and important. Jesus was attracted to celebrations. He encouraged other people, as many as 5,000 at one time, to eat and drink together. He began his public ministry at a wedding celebration in Cana, and soon after commented on the fact that some could not see past the image of him having a good time with others. "The Son of Man has come eating and drinking, and you say, 'Look, a glutton and a drunkard, a friend of tax-collectors and sinners!'" (Lk 7:34). Jesus gave us the beginnings of our eucharist during the celebration of the Passover, the Jewish feast marking God's victory over the harshness and oppression of slavery.

Sometimes people wonder how we can use the word "celebration" in reference to the eucharist, since in the eucharist we remember the events of Christ's death. Those who carry in their imaginations scenes such as those from the Mel Gibson movie *The Passion of the Christ* find the idea of celebrating eucharist difficult to understand. And it would be very difficult if that were the full extent of it. However, the key to understanding here is the end of the story: God's love reached through the power of death to raise Jesus to new life. Death had no more power over him, and by baptism we share in this new life of resurrection. In our eucharistic celebrations we give thanks for God's great love that gives us a share in this new life. That is why we can proclaim, "Dying, you destroyed our death. Rising, you restored our life. Lord Jesus, come in glory!" When we celebrate, we make our joy and hope tangible. No matter the occasion, whether it is an anniversary or a funeral, we can rejoice in faith because God's love has triumphed.

Think back to the last birthday party you attended. Picture the person whose life you were celebrating. Think of the other people who were there. Recall the event as it unfolded. No doubt a few stories were told, and it's likely gifts were given and received. A special ritual fire was probably lit (the birthday candles), and that particular ceremonial or ritual food and drink were shared. Expressing the meaning of this day and this particular person by well-known and practiced

ritual gestures is an integral part of the process of celebrating a birthday. So, too, with the eucharist. We tell
our stories of God's action in the Liturgy of the Word
and in the Eucharistic Prayer. We offer and others
receive our gifts—our very lives and our bread and
wine; we remember what God did for us in the death
and resurrection of Jesus, and we share the ritual food:
bread and wine transformed into his body and blood.
We mark the sacredness of these gestures with ritual
fire—candles, with special clothing in special colors
that help us say the meaning of this event. We can see,
taste, touch, and smell God's presence among us.

Many people have had one or more experiences
of God inviting them to eucharist as celebration. This
happened to Nancy during a retreat.

> This experience occurred on the sixth day of a
> ten-day silent retreat. The quotes are from my
> diary. At noon, I wrote, "Incredible day! Realize
> God and I are on holiday." This was my first long,
> silent retreat, and as an extrovert, I had been
> apprehensive about not talking to anyone but
> my spiritual director for ten full days. The reality,
> though, was wonderful. My whole being had
> slowed down, and I was much more sensitive to
> God's presence within and all around me. By the
> sixth day, I felt light and happy.
>
> I went for my spiritual direction session at
> 11:00 a.m. Hearing that I was in a celebratory
> mood, Sr. Debra suggested I pray through Jesus'
> giving us the eucharist, in the Ignatian way. This
> means using my imagination to enter into the
> scripture passage and make it as real as possible.
> When I returned from spiritual direction, I wrote,

"Very excited, anticipating. Even thinking about Jesus' gift to us, to me, brings strong gratitude."

Every afternoon, just before supper, the retreatants attended a liturgy led by the retreat team. I prayed through the events leading up to the Last Supper in gratitude, all afternoon, and was nearly at the part where Jesus takes bread and blesses it when it was time to go to the liturgy. I knew that tomorrow's liturgy would be a eucharistic celebration, but today's was to be a prayer service. So I thought, "I wonder if I can get a piece of bread and something to use for wine in the kitchen so that after supper I can continue my prayer experience with something I can really eat and drink?"

I walked into the chapel, feeling very open to Jesus, and stopped in my tracks. There on the small round table in the middle of our circle was a round loaf of bread with a cross cut into its top and a chalice. What a gift! I felt so overwhelmed with love and gratitude, I began to cry silently and cried on and off through the whole eucharist.

The next day, I asked Debra during spiritual direction, "How did that come to be?" She replied, "I was very surprised when Fr. Bob brought the bread and wine in. As a team, we had discussed when to have eucharist, and this was a day early. So afterward I asked him about the change. He told me that the idea came into his head quite strongly, so he took it as guidance from God. He had noticed you crying, so I told him what you had been doing all day. We rejoiced that our God gives each of us, personally, not only what we need, but also what will delight us. Actually, I was waiting for you to walk into the chapel. And the look on your face! You were stunned and delighted." By this time, I was crying again.

Some time after Nancy was given the gift of eucharist as celebration on that retreat, she began to worry about her worthiness to receive such gifts. She began to focus on the words we say just before we receive Christ's body and blood, "Lord, I am not worthy to receive you, but only say the word and I shall be healed." She wondered, "Does God want us to say this so that we can focus on our unworthiness?" This concern about being unworthy to receive God's gifts, or even to be in intimate relationship with God, is a common one and needs to be taken to God for refinement. If we believe that God wants us to focus on our unworthiness, our divine-human relationship will suffer. The view of God wanting us to dwell on our unworthiness doesn't match the description Jesus gave us about the divine personality. Our God is unconditionally loving, compassionate, merciful, and yet sometimes uses tough love for our good.

The word "unworthy" means having little value or merit. Those who believe they have little or no merit develop a low self-image and self-esteem. When we believe we have no merit, we will not believe that we have been created in God's image and likeness. Focusing on our unworthiness does not leave much time and energy to cherish and use the gifts God has given us. It also displaces what God has done for us, putting our own limitations in the centre of the picture. Some people think this is humility, but actually, it's the opposite.

Are we worthy of God's love? It seems a false question to ask since love is a gift, not an earned reward. We don't earn God's love; it is God's great gift to us. We are beloved children, period. So, why do we say, "I am not worthy," just before receiving? This statement comes from an experience Jesus had with a Roman centurion.

> After Jesus had finished all his sayings in the hearing of the people, he entered Capernaum. A centurion there had a slave whom he valued highly and who was ill and close to death. When he heard about Jesus, he sent some Jewish elders to him, asking him to come and heal his slave. When they came to Jesus, they appealed to him earnestly, saying, "He is worthy of having you do this for him, for he loves our people, and it is he who built our synagogue for us." And Jesus went with them, but when he was not far from the house, the centurion sent friends to say to him, "Lord, do not trouble yourself, for I am not worthy to have you come under my roof; therefore did I not presume to come to you. But only speak the word, and let my servant be healed. For I also am a man set under authority, with soldiers under me; and I say to one, 'Go,' and he goes, and to another, 'Come,' and he comes, and to my slave, 'Do this,' and the slave does it." When Jesus heard this, he was amazed at him, and turning to the crowd that followed him, he said, "I tell you, not even in Israel have I found such faith." When those who had been sent returned to the house, they found the slave in good health.

The centurion, leader of a hundred soldiers, would have been a man of power and prestige. The official

Roman policy was that the Jews were inferior beings. As a member of the occupying force, the centurion could have easily ordered Jesus to attend to him, sending a few of his soldiers to enforce his command. But this was a man who respected the Jews. He had built them a synagogue and he had Jewish friends— friends who could explain his needs to Jesus. Still, why didn't he come himself? There could be many reasons. Knowing that the centurion was sensitive to the cultural issues, he would have realized that a Jew often did not appreciate public contact with Romans. Also, he may not have spoken the language and may have needed interpreters to communicate with Jesus.

"I am not worthy to have you come under my roof," is a common statement in some Middle Eastern countries, for they value turning away praise. So the centurion was not debasing himself with these words. On the contrary, he was showing respect to Jesus. Then, after showing that he did not subscribe to the Roman belief that he was superior, the centurion demonstrated his faith. He knew, as a leader of soldiers, that his word had great authority. His followers obeyed and carried out his wishes immediately. Somehow he realized that Jesus had even more authority. His word was aligned with the healing power of the divine. The word of Jesus alone was enough to effect a cure. Jesus was amazed at the man's faith. And the slave was cured.

When we say, "Lord, I am not worthy to receive you, but only say the word and I shall be healed," we are putting ourselves in a position similar to the one the centurion saw for himself. He was a man of great faith who knew that Jesus could heal without being physically present, and his attitude bore witness to the respect he gave Jesus more than to how he saw himself. We can say these words with love and gratitude, giving ourselves to Christ as he gives us the gift of Himself. For as John Kavanaugh writes,

> In the sacrament of Christ's redemptive sacrifice, we also celebrate and consecrate our own gifts. We identify our lives, our labors, our passions, and our joys with the body, blood, history, and person of Jesus. (*Following Christ in a Consumer Society*, p. 145)

Feasting With God, Saints, and Angels

My name's Antonio. I love the many feast days of the church and try to attend Mass on as many of them as possible. I have found that learning more about the particular saints, angels, and aspects of God that we celebrate makes my spiritual life richer. I feel I have a lot of unseen friends surrounding me at all times, particularly during the eucharist. Of, course St. Anthony is special to me, although I'm getting to know many other members of our "cloud of witnesses" as I read the short biographies in the missalette. Sometimes I'm interested enough in a saint to read a book about them.

This story happened during the Feast of the Holy Trinity. During his homily, Fr. Vince talked about the Rule of Three, something I'd never heard of before. He said he was taught it in the novitiate. Brothers were encouraged to have relationships with two others, rather than developing a deep relationship with one other person. He said a couple, whether they are friends, brothers or sisters, might become too focused on each other, with little room in their hearts for others. Having two close friends teaches us to broaden our hearts. Fr. Vince spoke of the broadening of love that happens when a couple becomes a family, how the love expands. He then compared the Holy Trinity to a family.

As I sat listening prayerfully, God spoke into my heart. "You have not been opening your heart broadly to me." I was rather shocked because I have tried to be a faithful, God-loving Christian. And then I realized how I have been too narrow in my faith. Even though I've heard many times that the Three Persons of the Holy Trinity are equal, I usually directed my prayers to the Father. I'd been brought up in quite a traditional, patriarchal household where my father was definitely the head. Without realizing it, I had been viewing the Trinity in the same way. God was the head, Jesus, the son, came next, and the Holy Spirit was at the bottom of the hierarchy.

I wasn't listening to Fr. Vince any more. The awareness that I saw the Three Persons as unequal saddened me. And yet, as I expressed my remorse to God, I felt an answering delight. God was happy I had accepted the realization. So, I let go of my remorse, and, as I received the gift of Christ's body and blood, I asked for help to develop a deep relationship with each person of the Trinity, free from my earlier judgments. It took some time to shift from my habit of addressing Father God solely, yet as I did so, my relationship with God became better and better.

As well as celebrating the many feasts of our faith, the church year invites us to live with Christ through the story and meaning of his birth, public ministry, crucifixion, resurrection, and ascension. At the same time, we live along with story of the Jewish people as they interacted with God, and with the followers of Jesus as they spread out to share the Good News. There are many celebrations within this salvation history.

CELEBRATING WHAT GOD HAS DONE FOR US

Some people find the feast of the Assumption, celebrated on August 15, difficult to grasp. What does this really say about Mary? What does it say about us? This feast focused on Mary, whom God brings to the fullness of risen life with Christ, is, in fact, another celebration of the resurrection. The gospel proclaimed on that feast day is Mary's Magnificat, her great song of praise to God. It begins: "My soul magnifies the Lord, and my spirit rejoices in God, my Savior. For he has looked with favor on the lowliness of his servant. Surely, from now on all generations will call me blessed; for the Mighty One has done great things for me!"

One August 15, Bernadette was at Mass, listening to this gospel. When she heard those words, She was actually a bit envious of Mary until she began to think back over her own life. She examined the people and events of her life, and as she did so, she began to realize that Mary's words could be her own: God had done wonderful things in her life, too. That moment of insight transformed her own personal history, enabling her to see the stunning breadth of God's goodness, presence and love, even in dark and difficult times. At the same time, she discovered how true is our statement at the beginning of the eucharistic prayer: "It is right to give [God] thanks and praise."

EUCHARIST AND MIRACLES

A miracle is a wonderful, marvelous event that we view as an act of God, since it is contrary to the laws of nature. Frequently, the scripture readings during Mass describe miracles performed by Jesus, or occurring many centuries before his birth. They awe us and deepen our faith.

We may think miracles occurred only long ago and far away. God, however, is still in the miracle business. Many of the stories in this book seem miraculous. As the people told us of their experiences, they often said something like, "I didn't think healing was possible," or "There didn't seem to be a solution for my problem." And then God reached out in love, and the person received what he or she needed. Here are two more miracles that occurred during celebration of the eucharist. One of these miracles occurred in the 1990s, the other in the thirteenth century.

When I arrived as pastor of the small, rural community, the church had been closed for a few years, so I had a lot of work to do. As Holy Week approached, I realized these people had never experienced the whole Easter Triduum. I talked with them about it, and they responded with enthusiasm.

So on Holy Thursday the faith community turned out to celebrate Jesus' gift of the eucharist. Just before the final veneration, there is a procession to take the Blessed Sacrament to its place of repose. Often the procession winds up and down the aisles of the church, but in our tiny one, we had no aisles. I suggested we process outside four times around the building.

My dad, who was visiting, reminded me that it wasn't raining at that moment, but it had been raining all day, and the uncut grass around the church was two feet high. "We're going to get soaked," he said. I heard him, yet it felt right to do this. So, I led the people outside, and we sang a hymn as we circled the church in the dark. When we reentered the building, my dad came up to me and said, "My feet are dry!" It took a moment for his words to sink in. Then I looked at my own legs and feet. I was wearing open clogs, and there wasn't a drop of water on them. I had the whole congregation check their own shoes. Everyone had dry feet.

This miracle seemed to all of us to be a "yes" from God for our community. God was with us in a powerful, special way as we gathered together for the first Holy Thursday Mass in a long time.

And then, another miracle story.

> Eucharist is so important in my life, and I always
> eagerly await the special Feast Days. So here was
> Christmas approaching, and I was bedridden
> with a combination of old age and illness! I was
> pleased, though, that everyone was willing to
> leave me alone and attend the Christmas Eve
> service. Soon, they would be receiving Jesus.
> Of course, I knew that Jesus wasn't only in the
> church. He was also here with me. So I said to
> him, "See Lord, I am left here alone with You."
>
> And then, the miracle happened. I had a vision
> of the church. I heard the singing. I could see those
> I loved within and the liturgy unfolding! And the
> church was a mile away, so I shouldn't have been
> able to hear anything. What a celebration! What a
> Christmas gift you have given me, Lord, to delight
> me and bring me even closer to you. For that's the
> gift lovers give each other—themselves.
>
> I lay in my bed, watching and listening
> throughout the celebration. And when I told my
> loved ones upon their return what I had seen and
> heard, it was all correct.

Could you tell which was the modern miracle?
Yukon Bishop Gary Gordon told the first one to us.
It occurred in 1992 when he was sent as priest to St.
Theresa's Mission at Yakweakwioose First Nation.
St. Clare of Assisi, the foundress of the Poor Clares,
experienced the second miracle. No one can tell why
some people experience miracles and others do not,
or why they occur at the times they do. Miracles do
not happen based on a person's depth of faith or need.
Sometimes people miss the miracles that God sends

into their lives, maybe because they are not expecting them. Sometimes we can see an experience as miraculous as we look back in time at it.

Celebrating our God, who is not bound by the laws of nature, and rejoicing in the miracles we hear about in scripture and in everyday sacredness will deepen our faith and make us more sensitive to those God sends our way.

Closing Prayer

From Psalm 145, with responses by Nancy Reeves

I will extol you, my God and King,
and bless your name forever and ever.
Every day I will bless you,
and praise your name forever and ever.
Great is the Lord, and greatly to be praised;
his greatness is unsearchable (vv. 1–3).

Oh, God, I celebrate your presence in my life.
I celebrate the things that you have done for me.
I come to celebration of the eucharist
with love and gratitude for this great gift.

One generation shall laud your works to another,
and shall declare your mighty acts.
On the glorious splendor of your majesty,
and on your wondrous works, I will meditate.
The might of your awesome deeds shall be proclaimed,
and I will declare your greatness.

They shall celebrate the fame of your abundant
goodness,
and shall sing aloud of your righteousness
(vv. 4–7).

To hear of women and men from long ago
who loved you, and worshipped you,
and sometimes struggled with you,
makes my own spiritual path grow richer.
As I celebrate, I will be receptive to the lessons
you wish me to learn from these ancestors of mine.

The Lord is gracious and merciful,
slow to anger and abounding in steadfast love.
The Lord is good to all,
and his compassion is over all that he has made
(vv. 8–9).

Amen.

Questions to Journal or Discuss

1. What is your favorite feast day? What makes it so
   special to you?
2. Have you struggled with feeling unworthy before
   God? How has God helped you with this issue?

Spiritual Activity

Become aware of where we are in the church
year. Spend a little time reading or praying about an
upcoming feast day. You may wish to remember what

this feast has meant to you in the past. Then attend Mass on that feast day. Talking about it to family, friends, or other members of the congregation may spread the sense of celebration. During Mass, enter into the spirit of the feast as much as possible.

Afterward, ask yourself how being more informed about the feast affected your experience. Give thanks to God for this particular celebration.

* * *

From Linnea Good: "Psalm 100: Make A Joyful Noise."
Words and music at www.linneagood.com

EPILOGUE

So, have we done it? Have we discussed all the gifts God offers us through the eucharist? Of course not! Our infinite God gives infinite types of gifts, infinitely. For our finite book, however, we chose ten of the gifts that have been most frequently mentioned to us as authors, workshop presenters, and retreat leaders over the years.

We invite you to become aware of and to name other types of gifts as you receive them in the particular circumstances of your own faith story. Use the "Notes" pages at the back of this book to record your thoughts. Think of these gifts often and live richly from their blessings.

May God abundantly bless you and in all things be praised!

REFERENCES

Transformation

Searle, Mark. *Liturgy Made Simple*. Collegeville MN: Collegeville, MN: Liturgical Press, 1981.

Remembering

Durkin, Mary. *The Eucharist*. Chicago: The Thomas More Press, 1990.

Teilhard de Chardin, Pierre. *Hymn of the Universe*. New York: Harper & Row, 1961.

Thanksgiving

Deiss, Lucien. *It's the Lord's Supper: Eucharist of Christians*. New York: Paulist Press, 1976.

Reconciliation

Falardeau, Ernest. *One Bread and Cup: Source of Communion*. Wilmington, Delaware: Michael Glazier, 1987.

Turner, Paul. "Reconciliation Within the Eucharistic Liturgy," *Ministry & Liturgy* 33/10, December 2006–January 2007.

Healing

Reeves, Nancy C. *Found Through Loss: Healing Stories From Scripture and Everyday Sacredness*. Kelowna: Northstone, 1994. (Claire's story)

Rolheiser, Ron. "The Eucharist as Touch," *The Prairie Messenger*. Muenster, Saskatoon, October 13, 2002.

Nourishment

Bernier, Paul. *Bread Broken and Shared*. Notre Dame: Ave Maria Press, 1981.

Embrace

Merton, Thomas. *The Seven Storey Mountain*. New York: Harcourt, Brace, & Company, 1948.

Community

Huebsch, Bill. *Rethinking Sacraments: Holy Moments in Daily Living*. New London: Twenty-Third Publications, 1999.

Celebration

Kane, John A. *Transforming Your Life Through the Eucharist*. Manchester, New Hampshire: Sophia Institute Press, 1999.

Kavanaugh, John F. *Following Christ in a Consumer Society*. Maryknoll, New York: Orbis, 1991.

Notes

Notes

Notes

Bernadette Gasslein has been the editor of *Celebrate!*, a Canadian liturgy magazine for seventeen years. She has been involved in various liturgical and catechetical ministries, including four years as a Project Specialist with the National Office of Religious Education of the Canadian Conference of Catholic Bishops. She now leads workshops around North America. Bernadette holds a license in sacred theology with specialization in pastoral catechetics from the Institut Catholique de Paris. She is coordinator of liturgical life at St. Charles Parish in Edmonton, Alberta, where she and her husband live.

Nancy C. Reeves is a clinical psychologist, psychotherapist, spiritual director, best-selling author, and published poet. She works extensively in the areas of healing, transformation, and spiritual discernment. Nancy is an adjunct faculty member at the University of Victoria and guest lecturer at universities and colleges in Canada and the U.S. She has hosted workshops and retreats around the world and is the author of eight books. In 2002, Nancy was the recipient of the Victoria YM/YWCA Woman of Distinction Award—Health & Wellness category. She makes her home in Victoria, British Columbia.